THE ROYAL INSTITUTE
OF INTERNATIONAL AFFAIRS
London: Chatham House, St James's Square, S.W.1
New York: 542 Fifth Avenue, New York 19, N.Y.

Toronto   *Bombay*
Melbourne   *Wellington*   *Cape Town*
OXFORD UNIVERSITY PRESS

DOCUMENTS ON EUROPEAN RECOVERY AND DEFENCE

MARCH 1947 — APRIL 1949

London & New York
ROYAL INSTITUTE OF INTERNATIONAL
AFFAIRS

338.94

R 88

First published 1949

PRINTED IN GREAT BRITAIN
AT THE BROADWATER PRESS, WELWYN GARDEN CITY
HERTFORDSHIRE

PREFACE

This volume brings together for the first time between the same covers the basic documents on European recovery and defence which are most often in demand.

As the aim has been to produce a volume of moderate size and cost the selection in no way claims to give a complete documentation of the subject but is limited to official documents and pronouncements. It has thus been necessary to omit unofficial speeches and resolutions which played a no less vital part in stimulating public response, on both sides of the Atlantic, to the need for measures to bring about a greater degree of European unity. Among these are Mr Churchill's speech at Zurich in September 1946 and the resolutions passed at the Hague Conference in May 1948.

For the sake of consistency, certain minor typographical alterations have been made which in no way affect the sense.

CONTENTS

DOCUMENTS ON EUROPEAN RECOVERY AND DEFENCE

March 1947—April 1949

*

THE BENELUX CUSTOMS CONVENTION[1]

London, 5 September 1944

The Governments of His Majesty the King of the Belgians and Her Royal Highness the Grand Duchess of Luxembourg and The Government of Her Majesty the Queen of the Netherlands Desiring, in the hour of liberation of the territories of the Economic Union of Belgium-Luxembourg and of the Netherlands, to create the most favourable conditions for the eventual establishment of an economic union and for the restoration of economic activity, have determined to pursue such conditions through the medium of a Customs Convention, and to that end have agreed on the following provisions:

Article 1

The Economic Union of Belgium-Luxembourg and the Netherlands shall apply, on the entry of goods, identical customs rates in accordance with the schedule hereto appended and forming an integral part of the present Agreement.

Outside the duties referred to in this schedule, they may collect, on importation, excise duties—including entrance duties equivalent to excise duties—as well as all other taxes, in accordance with regulations in force in their respective territories; they reserve the right to modify the rates.

Article 2

There shall be only one collection of duty on the entry into the Economic Union of Belgium-Luxembourg of goods from the Netherlands, and likewise on the entry into the Netherlands of goods from the Economic Union of Belgium-Luxembourg, who may, on importation, collect excise duty.

On importation, the Economic Union of Belgium-Luxembourg may collect excise duty—including entrance duties equivalent to

---

[1] Hylkema, Edgar. *Bénélux, le chemin vers l'Unité économique.* Editions A. Pedone, 1948, pp. 181–186. Text as amended at The Hague, 14 March 1947. (*Translation.*)

I

excise duties—as well as all other taxes, in accordance with the regulations in force in their respective territories; they reserve the right to modify the rates.

Article 3

An Administrative Customs Council shall be formed, consisting of three Members from the Economic Union of Belgium-Luxembourg and three Members from the Netherlands. The principal Member from the Economic Union of Belgium-Luxembourg and the principal Member from the Netherlands will in turn act as Chairman of the Administrative Customs Council.

The Administrative Customs Council shall be responsible for proposing suitable measures for ensuring the unification of the legislative and statutory arrangements governing the collection of excise in the Economic Union of Belgium-Luxembourg and the Netherlands, and for their adaptation to the provisions of the present Agreement but without prejudice to the preliminary conditions in the schedule hereto appended.

Article 4

The Administrative Customs Council shall be assisted by a Commission on Customs Questions, consisting of two Members from the Economic Union of Belgium-Luxembourg and two Members from the Netherlands.

The Commission on Customs Questions, when approached by the competent Ministers, shall settle the differences arising out of the application of the legal or statutory conditions resulting from the present Agreement.

The Commission shall communicate its decisions to the competent Ministers, each of whom shall ensure the execution of those falling within his competence.

Article 5

A Council on Economic Union shall be formed, consisting of three Members from the Economic Union of Belgium-Luxembourg and three Members from the Netherlands. The principal Member from the Economic Union of Belgium-Luxembourg and the principal Member from the Netherlands shall act in turn as Chairman.

The Council on Economic Union shall have the following objects:

(a) To give an opinion for the benefit of the competent authorities of the Economic Union of Belgium-Luxembourg and of the Netherlands on all measures contemplated by the Economic Union of Belgium-Luxembourg and the Netherlands with a view to regulating, with or without accessory duties or taxes, imports, exports, and

2

transit, especially by instituting restrictions of an economic nature, licences, quotas, special licence rights, and administrative taxes;

(b) To co-ordinate the measures referred to above with a view to establishing as far as possible a common system in the Economic Union of Belgium-Luxembourg and in the Netherlands;

(c) To ensure the administration of quotas for imports, exports, and transit, which shall be common to the Economic Union of Belgium-Luxembourg and the Netherlands;

(d) To give an opinion for the benefit of the competent authorities of the Economic Union of Belgium-Luxembourg on all measures concerning grants or subsidies to production which the contracting parties may propose to make.

Article 6

A Commercial Agreements Council shall be formed, consisting of three Members from the Economic Union of Belgium-Luxembourg and three Members from the Netherlands. The principal Member from the Economic Union of Belgium-Luxembourg and the principal Member from the Netherlands shall act in turn as Chairman of the Commercial Agreements Council.

The Commercial Agreements Council shall ensure as far as possible the co-ordination of arrangements concerning existing relations with third-party States.

Article 7

These common measures as set out in Articles 3, 5, and 6 of the Agreement shall be fixed by the competent Ministers sitting for the Economic Union of Belgium-Luxembourg and for the Netherlands. They shall be submitted by them for the approval of the competent governmental or legal authorities.

Article 8

The present Agreement shall be ratified and shall come into force on the first day of the third month after the exchange of the instruments of ratification.

It may be terminated at any time, subject to one year's notice.

It shall in any event cease to be effective on the coming into force of the long-term economic union which the contracting parties propose to conclude.

Article 9

Until such time as instruments of ratification are exchanged the Convention shall come provisionally into effect immediately the

3

Belgian and Netherlands Governments are re-established in their territories; nevertheless either of the afore-named shall be entitled to terminate it any any time, subject to six months' notice.

In witness whereof the Plenipotentiaries, having been duly authorized for that purpose, have signed the present Agreement and have affixed thereto their seals.

DUNKIRK TREATY

TREATY OF ALLIANCE AND MUTUAL ASSISTANCE BETWEEN HIS MAJESTY IN RESPECT OF THE UNITED KINGDOM OF GREAT BRITAIN AND NORTHERN IRELAND AND THE PRESIDENT OF THE FRENCH REPUBLIC[1]

Dunkirk, 4 March 1947

His Majesty The King of Great Britain, Ireland and the British Dominions beyond the Seas, Emperor of India, and
The President of the French Republic,

Desiring to confirm in a Treaty of Alliance the cordial friendship and close association of interests between the United Kingdom and France;

Convinced that the conclusion of such a Treaty will facilitate the settlement in a spirit of mutual understanding of all questions arising between the two countries;

Resolved to co-operate closely with one another as well as with the other United Nations in preserving peace and resisting aggression, in accordance with the Charter of the United Nations[2] and in particular with Articles 49, 51, 52, 53 and 107 thereof;

Determined to collaborate in measures of mutual assistance in the event of any renewal of German aggression, while considering most desirable the conclusion of a treaty between all the Powers having responsibility for action in relation to Germany with the object of preventing Germany from becoming again a menace to peace;

Having regard to the Treaties of Alliance and Mutual Assistance which they have respectively concluded with the Union of Soviet Socialist Republics[3];

Intending to strengthen the economic relations between the two countries to their mutual advantage and in the interests of general prosperity;

Have decided to conclude a Treaty with these objects and have appointed as their Plenipotentiaries:

[Here follow the Signatures]

---

[1] Cmd. 7217.
[2] 'Treaty Series No. 67 (1946),' Cmd. 7015.
[3] 'Treaty Series No. 2 (1942),' Cmd. 6376 (Anglo-Soviet Treaty).

5

who, having communicated their Full Powers, found in good and due form, have agreed as follows:—

Article I

Without prejudice to any arrangements that may be made, under any Treaty concluded between all the Powers having responsibility for action in relation to Germany under Article 107 of the Charter of the United Nations, for the purpose of preventing any infringements by Germany of her obligations with regard to disarmament and de-militarisation and generally of ensuring that Germany shall not again become a menace to peace, the High Contracting Parties will, in the event of any threat to the security of either of them arising from the adoption by Germany of a policy of aggression or from action by Germany designed to facilitate such a policy, take, after consulting with each other and where appropriate with the other Powers having responsibility for action in relation to Germany, such agreed action (which so long as the said Article 107 remains operative shall be action under that Article) as is best calculated to put an end to this threat.

Article II

Should either of the High Contracting Parties become again involved in hostilities with Germany,

either in consequence of an armed attack, within the meaning of Article 51 of the Charter of the United Nations, by Germany against that Party,

or as a result of agreed action taken against Germany under Article I of this Treaty,

or as a result of enforcement action taken against Germany by the United Nations Security Council,

the other High Contracting Party will at once give the High Contracting Party so involved in hostilities all the military and other support and assistance in his power.

Article III

In the event of either High Contracting Party being prejudiced by the failure of Germany to fulfil any obligation of an economic character imposed on her as a result of the Instrument of Surrender or arising out of any subsequent settlement, the High Contracting Parties will consult with each other and where appropriate with the other Powers having responsibility for action in relation to Germany, with a view to taking agreed action to deal with the situation.

6

Article IV

Bearing in mind the interests of the other members of the United Nations, the High Contracting Parties will by constant consultation on matters affecting their economic relations with each other take all possible steps to promote the prosperity and economic security of both countries and thus enable each of them to contribute more effectively to the economic and social objectives of the United Nations.

Article V

(1) Nothing in the present Treaty should be interpreted as derogating in any way from the obligations devolving upon the High Contracting Parties from the provisions of the Charter of the United Nations or from any special agreements concluded in virtue of Article 43 of the Charter.

(2) Neither of the High Contracting Parties will conclude any alliance or take part in any coalition directed against the other High Contracting Party; nor will they enter into any obligation inconsistent with the provisions of the present Treaty.

Article VI

(1) The present Treaty is subject to ratification and the instruments of ratification will be exchanged in London as soon as possible.

(2) It will come into force immediately on the exchange of the instruments of ratification and will remain in force for a period of fifty years.

(3) Unless either of the High Contracting Parties gives to the other notice in writing to terminate it at least one year before the expiration of this period, it will remain in force without any specified time limit, subject to the right of either of the High Contracting Parties to terminate it by giving to the other in writing a year's notice of his intention to do so.

In witness whereof the above-mentioned Plenipotentiaries have signed the present Treaty and affixed thereto their seals.

Done in Dunkirk the fourth day of March 1947, in duplicate in English and French, both texts being equally authentic.

(L.S.)	ERNEST BEVIN
(L.S.)	DUFF COOPER
(L.S.)	BIDAULT
(L.S.)	R. MASSIGLI

SPEECH BY MR GEORGE MARSHALL

Harvard University, 5 June 1947

I need not tell you gentlemen that the world situation is very serious. That must be apparent to all intelligent people. I think one difficulty is that the problem is one of such enormous complexity that the very mass of facts presented to the public by press and radio make it exceedingly difficult for the man in the street to reach a clear appraisement of the situation. Furthermore, the people of this country are distant from the troubled areas of the earth and it is hard for them to comprehend the plight and consequent reactions of the long-suffering peoples, and the effect of those reactions on their governments in connection with our efforts to promote peace in the world.

In considering the requirements for the rehabilitation of Europe, the physical loss of life, the visible destruction of cities, factories, mines, and railroads was correctly estimated, but it has become obvious during recent months that this visible destruction was probably less serious than the dislocation of the entire fabric of European economy. For the past ten years conditions have been highly abnormal. The feverish preparation for war and the more feverish maintenance of the war effort engulfed all aspects of national economies. Machinery has fallen into disrepair or is entirely obsolete. Under the arbitrary and destructive Nazi rule, virtually every possible enterprise was geared into the German war machine. Long-standing commercial ties, private institutions, banks, insurance companies, and shipping companies disappeared, through loss of capital, absorption through nationalization, or by simple destruction. In many countries, confidence in the local currency has been severely shaken. The breakdown of the business structure of Europe during the war was complete. Recovery has been seriously retarded by the fact that two years after the close of hostilities a peace settlement with Germany and Austria has not been agreed upon. But even given a more prompt solution of these difficult problems, the rehabilitation of the economic structure of Europe quite evidently will require a much longer time and greater effort than had been foreseen.

There is a phase of this matter which is both interesting and serious. The farmer has always produced the foodstuffs to exchange with the city dweller for the other necessities of life. This division of labour is the basis of modern civilization. At the present time it is threatened with breakdown. The town and city industries are not producing adequate goods to exchange with the food-producing farmer. Raw materials and fuel are in short supply. Machinery is lacking or worn out. The farmer or the peasant cannot find the goods for sale which he desires to purchase. So the sale of his farm produce for money which he cannot use seems to him an unprofitable transaction. He, therefore, has withdrawn many fields from crop cultivation and is using them for grazing. He feeds more grain to stock and finds for himself and his family an ample supply of food, however short he may be on clothing and the other ordinary gadgets of civilization. Meanwhile people in the cities are short of food and fuel. So the governments are forced to use their foreign money and credits to procure these necessities abroad. This process exhausts funds which are urgently needed for reconstruction. Thus a very serious situation is rapidly developing which bodes no good for the world. The modern system of the division of labour upon which the exchange of products is based is in danger of breaking down.

The truth of the matter is that Europe's requirements for the next three or four years of foreign food and other essential products— principally from America—are so much greater than her present ability to pay that she must have substantial additional help or face economic, social, and political deterioration of a very grave character.

The remedy lies in breaking the vicious circle and restoring the confidence of the European people in the economic future of their own countries and of Europe as a whole. The manufacturer and the farmer throughout wide areas must be able and willing to exchange their products for currencies the continuing value of which is not open to question.

Aside from the demoralizing effect on the world at large and the possibilities of disturbances arising as a result of the desperation of the people concerned, the consequences to the economy of the United States should be apparent to all. It is logical that the United States should do whatever it is able to do to assist in the return of normal economic health in the world, without which there can be no political stability and no assured peace. Our policy is directed not against any country or doctrine but against hunger, poverty, desperation, and chaos. Its purpose should be the revival of a working economy in the world so as to permit the emergence of political and social conditions in which free institutions can exist. Such assistance, I am convinced, must not be on a piecemeal basis as crises develop. Any assistance that this Government may render in the future should provide a cure rather than a mere palliative. Any

B
9

government that is willing to assist in the task of recovery will find full co-operation, I am sure, on the part of the United States Government. Any government which manoeuvres to block the recovery of other countries cannot expect help from us. Furthermore, governments, political parties, or groups which seek to perpetuate human misery in order to profit therefrom politically or otherwise will encounter the opposition of the United States.

It is already evident that, before the United States Government can proceed much further in its efforts to alleviate the situation and help start the European world on its way to recovery, there must be some agreement among the countries of Europe as to the requirements of the situation and the part those countries themselves will take in order to give proper effect to whatever action might be undertaken by this Government. It would be neither fitting or efficacious for this Government to undertake to draw up unilaterally a programme designed to place Europe on its feet economically. This is the business of the Europeans. The initiative, I think, must come from Europe. The role of this country should consist of friendly aid in the drafting of a European programme and of later support of such a programme so far as it may be practical for us to do so. The programme should be a joint one, agreed to by a number of, if not all, European nations.

An essential part of any successful action on the part of the United States is an understanding on the part of the people of America of the character of the problem and the remedies to be applied. Political passion and prejudice should have no part. With foresight, and a willingness on the part of our people to face up to the vast responsibility which history has clearly placed upon our country, the difficulties I have outlined can and will be overcome.

REPORT OF THE COMMITTEE OF EUROPEAN ECONOMIC CO-OPERATION

(Official United States Summary)[1]

In response to the speech of Secretary of State Marshall, made at Harvard on 5 June 1947, representatives of sixteen European nations met in Paris beginning on 12 July to examine their prospective requirements and resources during the period 1948–51 and to formulate an economic recovery program. The countries represented were Austria, Belgium, Denmark, France, Greece, Iceland, Italy, Luxembourg, the Netherlands, Norway, Portugal, Sweden, Switzerland, Turkey, and the United Kingdom; western Germany was also included in the analysis and calculations of the Committee.

ORGANIZATION

To prepare the CEEC report, a number of technical committees were set up, dealing with food and agriculture, fuel and power, iron and steel, transport (internal and maritime), timber, and manpower, as well as a balance of payments committee and a committee of financial experts. The food and agriculture committee considered problems of agricultural machinery and fertilizer, in addition to those of food and feedstuffs. The fuel and power committee considered the problems of coal, electricity, and petroleum products, and, in addition, those relating to mining machinery, electrical equipment, and petroleum equipment.

The first concern was to obtain the necessary statistical information. For this purpose, the technical committees sent questionnaires to each of the participating countries and western Germany, requesting data for their respective commodities on total requirements, production plans, expected exports, and required imports. The Balance of Payments Committee used the findings of the technical committees in their respective fields, and also obtained information by questionnaire on anticipated payments and receipts of all other items; these data were combined into an over-all statement of the anticipated surplus and deficit of the participating countries and western Germany with the rest of the world.

[1] From *The European Recovery Program: Basic Documents and Background Information* (80th Congress, 1st Session: Senate: Document No. 111), Washington 1947.

11

ASSUMPTIONS

In obtaining the necessary basic data through questionnaires, the technical committees requested the governments of the respective countries to adopt certain assumptions, and presumably the same assumptions were followed by the committees in the assessment and correlation of the statistics and information submitted. These assumptions were that: (1) Foreign exchange to pay for essential imports would be available; (2) consumption standards would not exceed those which the respective countries expect to be able to maintain after 1951; (3) import requirements would be consistent with the aim of reducing the dollar deficit of the countries by 1951 to that manageable thereafter without special external assistance; and (4) production and consumption would be at levels consistent with 'high and stable employment'. It should also be pointed out that for some commodities expected to be in short supply relative to import needs, such as cereals, meat, and timber, the data used by the committees correspond to estimated available supplies rather than to total import requirements. Finally, because of the difficulty of accurately predicting prices, the technical committees calculated all values on the basis of prices prevailing on 1 July 1947 'in the most likely outside source of supply'.

For the purpose of developing a balance of payments, and thereby determining the deficit in means of payment of the participating countries and western Germany with the rest of the world, certain further assumptions were adopted which relate particularly to this section of the CEEC report. These assumptions were that: (1) Production in the participating countries will increase greatly; (2) the imports required for increased production will be available; (3) an increasing part of the necessary imports can be obtained from eastern Europe and south-east Asia; (4) the goods which the participating countries produce for export can be sold to the Western Hemisphere and to the rest of the world; (5) the non-participating countries will so far as necessary be able to pay for goods imported from the participating countries in dollars; and (6) there will be a progressive reduction in the price of imports into the participating countries in relation to the price of exports from those countries.

THE RECOVERY PROGRAM

The report of the CEEC outlines a program of economic recovery for the sixteen participating nations and western Germany based on four lines of action:

(1) A production program in the participating countries and western Germany, designed in general to restore agricultural produc-

12

tion to pre-war levels by 1951 and to increase industrial production by 1951 somewhat above the 1938 levels;

(2) The creation and maintenance of internal financial stability;

(3) The development of economic co-operation among the participating countries in production, in joint development of resources, in trade, in the movement of persons and transport, and in the establishment of a continuing organization;

(4) A solution of the dollar deficit of the participating countries, particularly by the expansion of exports.

IMPORT REQUIREMENTS

To carry out the production program, the CEEC report emphasizes that the sixteen European nations and western Germany will require a large and uninterrupted flow of goods from the rest of the world, and in particular from the American continent. The total value of the goods required from foreign sources during the period 1948–51 is estimated to be 57·4 billion dollars, distributed fairly evenly among the four years. In addition, requirements of dollar shipping are estimated to be 1·7 billion dollars.

Because of the loss of supplies from customary pre-war sources, the sixteen European nations expect to depend heavily on the United States and other American countries for imports of needed commodities. During the period 1948–51, it is estimated that 61 per cent of total commodity requirements will come from the Western Hemisphere (35 per cent from the United States and 26 per cent from other American countries), compared with about 45 per cent in pre-war years. Assuming a gradual resumption of imports of goods from customary pre-war sources such as eastern Europe and south-east Asia, however, the share of total imports from the United States is estimated to decrease from 43 per cent in 1948 to 30 per cent in 1951; on the other hand, the share of imports from non-American countries is estimated to increase from 34 per cent in 1948 to 43 per cent in 1951. Total import requirements of the participating countries and western Germany, by area, are shown in table I.

In terms of value, requirements of the participating countries and western Germany for foreign goods are expected to consist primarily of food, fuel, and fertilizer, which together are estimated to amount to 73 per cent of total imports during the four years 1948–51. Imports from the United States are anticipated to be chiefly food and fertilizer (28 per cent of total imports from the United States); fuel (14 per cent); other raw materials (27 per cent); and various types of equipment (25 per cent). Import requirements from other countries in the Western Hemisphere are expected to consist principally of food and fertilizer (59 per cent) and other raw materials (35 per cent). Estimated import requirements of the participating countries from the American continent, 1948–51, are shown in table II.

Assuming the fulfilment of the import requirements of the participating countries and western Germany, the means of payment for those imports of goods and services, without special outside assistance, will be only partially available. The stated purpose of the recovery program outlined by the participating countries is to reduce steadily the annual deficit in means of payment during 1948–51 to that manageable thereafter without special external aid.

The size of the deficit in means of payment is tentatively estimated in the CEEC report by the Balance of Payments Committee. On the basis of certain assumptions mentioned above, the Committee estimates that the total deficit of the participating countries will be reduced from 8·3 billion dollars in 1948 to 1·6 billion dollars in 1951, and will amount to 19·6 billion dollars for the four-year period 1948–51. The year-to-year reduction is to be accomplished to a great extent by increasing exports of goods which are expected to be valued at 6·5 billion dollars in 1948 and 10·8 billion dollars in 1951.

The dollar deficit with the American Continent, which is emphasized in the CEEC report, is estimated at 22·4 billion dollars for the period 1948–51, decreasing from 8 billion dollars in 1948 to 3·4 billion dollars in 1951; 16·5 billion dollars is expected to be with the United States and 5·9 billion dollars with other countries in the Western Hemisphere. As against the dollar deficit, a surplus in means of payment with the rest of the world for the period 1948–51 is estimated at 2·8 billion dollars which, if dollars are available in the trade with the rest of the world, is expected to reduce the total deficit of the participating countries to 19·6 billion dollars. The Committee emphasizes that these statistics no more than indicate the prospective size of the deficit in means of payment, and do not necessarily correspond to the amount of special assistance which will be required. If imports of capital equipment are financed by loans from the International Bank, the total deficit could be reduced by as much as an estimated 3·1 billion dollars. Loans from other sources as well as the expenditure of other financial resources by the participating countries would further reduce the deficit. On the other hand, if the sixteen European countries are unable to earn dollars for their exports, the anticipated surplus with the rest of the world could not be employed to reduce the dollar deficit with the Western Hemisphere. The estimated net balance of payments of the participating countries, indicating deficit or surplus, is shown in table III.

EUROPEAN SELF-HELP

In addition to unilateral and co-operative action on the part of each of the sixteen western European countries to attain the projected levels of production and to solve the problem of the dollar deficit, the CEEC report sets forth certain fields wherein additional mutual effort would be of benefit to the recovery program. First the Committee of Economic Co-operation points out that for 'increased production in the area to make its full contribution to the restoration of the European economy and the reduction of abnormal demands on the rest of the world, it must be accompanied by a freer movement of goods and services within Europe itself'. Consequently, the participating countries resolved to remove as soon as possible abnormal restrictions on their mutual trade and, as between themselves and the rest of the world, to work toward the adoption of a multilateral trading system envisaged in the draft charter for an international trade organization. To the end of expanding their mutual trade, thirteen of the sixteen participating countries created a study group to examine the problems involved and the steps to be taken in the formation of a customs union between themselves.

The Committee also recommended collective action in certain specific fields. Among these were the co-operative exploitation of electric power resources (summarized below in the section on electric power), standardization of equipment such as mining machinery and freight cars, pooling arrangements of freight cars, and interchange of information on the development and modernization of steel industries to avoid duplication and over-expansion.

COMMITTEE OF FINANCIAL EXPERTS

The report of the Committee of Financial Experts recognizes the necessity of internal financial and monetary stability to the success of the European recovery programme. At the Paris Conference, declarations were made by representatives of a number of countries, including Austria, Belgium, Denmark, France, Greece, Italy, the Netherlands, Norway, Portugal, Sweden, Switzerland, and the United Kingdom, relative to monetary conditions within their countries and the steps which their governments proposed to take to achieve internal financial stability. To this end the Committee suggested that it would be of assistance if supplementary foreign resources specifically intended to raise the gold and dollar reserves of various countries were made available. Although a precise calculation was not attempted, the total amount of such financial assistance required was tentatively estimated at 3 billion dollars.

After internal financial stabilization has been achieved and can be successfully maintained, the sixteen European countries have pledged themselves to make their currencies convertible, as defined in the articles of agreement of the International Monetary Fund, at appropriate rates of exchange. In addition, the Committee considered the problems of making more flexible inter-European payments agreements to the end of assisting the development of their mutual trade.

REPORTS OF THE TECHNICAL COMMITTEES

1. Food and Agriculture

The food-production program of the participating countries and western Germany includes the restoration of pre-war levels of production of bread grains, coarse grains, fats and oils, and milk by the crop year 1950–51. The output of sugar by 1950–51 is expected to be 15 per cent larger than in pre-war years, while the production of meat is anticipated to reach only 90 per cent of pre-war levels. Because of the increase in population (estimated at 278 million persons in 1951, compared with 270 million in 1947 and 246 million in 1938), the consumption of food per capita by 1950–51 is expected to be still somewhat below pre-war levels. Specifically, per capita consumption of bread grains by 1950–51 is expected to be 7 per cent below pre-war levels; sugar, 11 per cent; fats and oils, 12 per cent; and meat, 20 per cent. Consumption of potatoes, however, is expected to be about 3 per cent above pre-war levels by 1950–51. During the four years of the program, a large increase in the output of agricultural machinery and fertilizers is also planned. Production of tractors is expected to increase from 182,000 in 1947–48 to 380,000 in 1950–51, production of other agricultural machinery from 922,000 metric tons to 1·5 million tons, and production of fertilizer from 3·2 million tons to 6·2 million tons.

The report emphasizes the need for large imports of food to maintain standards of consumption in the participating countries during the period production is being restored, and also the need for substantial imports of fertilizers and machinery to achieve the planned levels of production. Total import requirements of these goods for the four crop years 1947–48 to 1950–51 are estimated at 32·7 billion dollars; of this amount, imports of food and feedstuffs are estimated at 31·3 billion dollars, fertilizers at 450 million dollars, and tractors and machinery at 950 million dollars. Sources of these imports are considered to be as follows: Dependent overseas territories, 6·2 billion dollars; United States, 7·6 billion dollars; other Western Hemisphere countries, 8·8 billion dollars; and the rest of the world, 10·1 billion dollars.

2. Coal

The participating countries and western Germany plan to expand the production of coal from 439 million metric tons in 1948 to 584 million tons in 1951, or to 6 per cent greater than the 1938 output. To achieve this goal, a substantial program of manufacturing coal-mining machinery within the participating countries is planned, as well as special inducements in housing and pay to assure an adequate labor force. Necessary imports of coal-mining machinery, amounting to about 6 per cent of total machinery requirements, are estimated at 220 million dollars for the four years 1948–51.

During the period of the recovery program, requirements for solid fuel are expected to increase from 535 million tons in 1948 to 620 million tons (65 million tons, or 12 per cent, above the 1938 level) in 1951. These requirements for 1948–51 exceed anticipated production by a total of 187 million tons. To supply this deficit, import requirements from the United States are estimated at 86 million metric tons, valued at 774 million dollars, and requirements from Poland and other countries at 101 million tons, valued at 1,515 million dollars. After 1951 it is expected that imports from the United States, which are uneconomic because of the long haul, will not be required.

3. Electric Power

The annual production of electric power in the participating countries and western Germany, which is estimated at 170 billion kilowatt-hours in 1947, is now greater than the 1938 output of 130 billion kilowatt-hours. The total requirements of electric power, however, are expected to increase markedly during the recovery period, from 178 billion kilowatt-hours in 1947 to 243 billion kilowatt-hours in 1951. Consequently the participating countries plan a series of so-called national expansion programs intended to increase the total generating capacity of electric power plants from 43·4 million kilowatts in 1947 to 65·5 million kilowatts in 1951, or an increase of about 50 per cent; the output in 1951 expected from this expanded plant is estimated to be 237 billion kilowatt-hours, or about 2 per cent less than estimated requirements. To conserve coal, the participating countries plan to establish hydro-electric plants where possible; of the total estimated increase in annual power output between 1947 and 1951 (67 billion kilowatt-hours), hydro-electric power accounts for 30 billion kilowatt-hours, which is estimated to be the equivalent of about 20 million tons of coal. In addition to the national programs, a so-called international program is planned, involving the establishment of nine electric power plants with a combined capacity of 2·3 million kilowatts in the countries of France, Italy, Switzerland, Austria, and western Germany. Six of the plants will be hydro-electric, one geothermic, and two will use brown coal. The average annual output from these plants is expected to be 6·6 billion kilowatt-hours; it is anticipated that most of the plant could be completed within four years, and would serve to make up at least part of the electric-power deficit.

The participating countries plan to supply a large part of the equipment and supplies necessary for the projected expansion of generating capacity. The 'national' programs are estimated to cost 5 billion dollars, of which 300 million dollars represents specialized equipment required from the United States. The supplementary 'international' program is estimated to cost 315 million dollars, of which equipment from the United States is expected to amount to 200 million dollars.

4. Petroleum Products

Total requirements for petroleum products in the participating countries and western Germany are expected to increase materially during the period of the recovery program, amounting to an estimated 68·7 million metric tons in 1951, compared with 53·0 million tons in 1948; requirements in 1938 amounted to 33·3 million tons. Increased production of crude oil at home, in dependent territories, and in other overseas areas is planned, as well as the expansion of refining facilities within the participating countries to two and a half times the pre-war level, or sufficient to process 31·4 million tons of crude in 1951 compared with 11·3 million tons in 1947 and 13 million tons in 1938.

During the period 1948–51, total import requirements of crude oil are estimated at 87 million metric tons, valued at 1·2 billion dollars; of this, 46 million tons, valued at 580 million dollars, is expected to be needed from sources requiring payment in dollars. Imports of refined products are estimated at 156 million tons, valued at 3·5 billion dollars; of this amount, 62 million tons, valued at 1·9 billion dollars, is expected to be needed from dollar sources. Total equipment requirements for the four-year period are calculated at 1·8 billion dollars; of this amount, 0·6 billion dollars are expected to consist of machinery and supplies from the United States.

5. Iron and Steel

The production program of the participating countries and western Germany relating to iron and steel is planned to be one primarily of modernization and capacity use of existing facilities. Expanded production in the sixteen participating countries alone is expected to increase the output from 26·8 million tons of crude steel in 1947 to 42·7 million tons in 1951; output of crude steel in those countries in 1938 amounted to 24·7 million tons. Production of steel in western Germany, controlled by the level of industry plan, is limited to greatly less than the 1938 output; hence, the planned output of the participating countries and western Germany combined amounts to 55·4 million tons of crude steel in 1951 compared with 30·3 million tons in 1947 and 45·5 million tons in 1938.

The production program in iron and steel is based on the assumption of full supplies of raw materials, as are the other production programs formulated in the CEEC report. It appears, however, that there may be deficits in the supply of some steel-making materials. The most serious potential deficit is considered to be in the supply of coke. It is hoped that coke shortages can be overcome by increased imports of coking coal, chiefly from the United States, by diverting coke from non-metallurgical uses, and by reducing coke requirements through the use of richer iron ores. Other potential shortages of steel-making materials relate to scrap, manganese ore, and, in 1951, to rich iron ore. These anticipated shortages, excluding consideration of coke deficits, may reduce production during 1948–51 to about 5 per cent below the planned levels; shortages of coke amounting to 4 million tons out of total requirements of 65·6 million tons in 1948, for example, would reduce crude steel production about 15 per cent below that planned.

To achieve the planned production of crude steel, to fully utilize steel-finishing capacity, and to supply certain requirements of finished products (principally tinplate and sheet), import requirements for the period 1948–51 are estimated as follows: Raw materials (excluding coke), 446 million dollars; crude and semi-finished steel, 662 million dollars; finished steel, 330 million dollars; and equipment, 400 million dollars. Total import requirements of these products are valued at 1,838 million dollars; of this amount, 1,565 million dollars, or 85 per cent, is expected to be needed from the United States.

6. Timber

The production of timber in the participating countries and western Germany in 1951 is expected to supply about 60 per cent of softwood requirements, 70 per cent of hardwood requirements, and 80 per cent of the requirements for pit props, pulpwood, and poles. Available supplies of timber, however, are not considered sufficient to furnish all the requirements for softwood, or for pit props, pulpwood, and poles. Timber expected to be available is estimated at 2·4 billion dollars during the four-year period 1948–51. Imports of equipment deemed necessary in order to meet the production program of the participating countries are estimated at 57 million dollars. Of imports of both timber and equipment, about 17 per cent is expected to be available from the United States, 25 per cent from the other American countries, and 58 per cent from other non-participating countries.

7. Inland Transport

The participating countries consider it necessary to improve their inland transportation system so that the railways can carry 854 million metric tons of cargo in 1951 compared with 738 million tons in 1948, and so that the waterways can carry 174 million tons in 1951 compared with 122 million tons in 1948. Except for deficiencies in railway stock, however, the participating countries expect to be able to supply their own equipment needs. Import requirements of railway stock, amounting to 103,000 freight cars and 2,600 passenger cars for the period 1948–51, are estimated to cost 479 million dollars; requirements of special equipment for Greece are estimated to be 11 million dollars. The United States is expected to be the only possible source of these imports.

8. Maritime Transport

The sixteen participating countries plan, by the end of 1951, to have a maritime transport capacity of 39·2 million dead-weight tons of dry-cargo shipping and 14·4 million tons of tankers. The program involves not only replacement of large losses of cargo ships suffered during the war but also some expansion to make up in part the loss to world shipping of the German and Japanese fleets. The shipping capacity of the sixteen participating countries in 1938 amounted to 36·1 million tons of dry-cargo shipping and 10·1 million tons of tankers; the German fleet included 5·9 million tons of dry-cargo shipping and 0·4 million tons of tankers. To carry out the expansion program, the countries propose to purchase from the United States 3 million dead-weight tons of shipping at an estimated cost of 300 million dollars, in addition to 500 million dollars already purchased, and to supply the remainder by new construction.

During the replacement and expansion period, the total carrying capacity of the participating countries will be insufficient to meet their requirements and those of western Germany. To make up the deficit, the use of substantial, but decreasing, amounts of dollar tonnage for dry-cargo shipping are considered necessary. These requirements are estimated to decrease from 500 million dollars in 1948 to 130 million dollars in 1951; total costs are expected to be 1,220 million dollars. On the other hand, requirements for dollar tonnage of tankers are expected to increase, as imports of petroleum increase, from 70 million dollars in 1948 to 180 million dollars in 1951; total cost of tankers are estimated to be 485 million dollars.

9. Manpower

Combined labor requirements of the sixteen participating countries and western Germany for agriculture and industry are estimated at about 680,000 persons. Present labor resources are considered to be principally 2 million unemployed Italian workers and 500,000 displaced persons. Immigration of labor is expected, therefore, to supply labor requirements in terms of numbers. The manpower committee pointed out, however, that requirements for various types of skilled labor, such as miners, exceed the numbers of skilled workers available. Consequently, programs of vocational training are required in the participating countries.

TABLE I

Total import requirements of participating countries (excluding dependent territories) and western Germany, by area.
(In billions of U.S. dollars)

	1948	1949	1950	1951	Total
United States	6·0	5·3	4·8	4·3	20·4
Other American countries	3·2	3·9	3·8	3·9	14·8
Total, Western Hemisphere	9·2	9·2	8·6	8·2	35·2
Rest of world	4·7	5·4	5·9	6·2	22·2
Total, all countries	13·9	14·6	14·5	14·4	57·4
Dollar shipping	·6	·4	·4	·3	1·7

TABLE II

Estimated import requirements of the participating countries (excluding dependent territories) and western Germany from the American Continent for the period 1948–51.
(In billions of U.S. dollars)

	United States	Other American countries	Total
Food, feedstuffs, and fertilizers	5·6	8·7	14·3
Coal	·7	—	·7
Petroleum products[1]	2·2	—.	2·2
Iron and steel	1·2	·1	1·3
Timber	·4	·6	1·0
Equipment	5·1	·1	5·2
Other imports[2]	5·2	5·3	10·5
Total imports	20·4	14·8	35·2
Shipping services	1·7	—	1·7

[1] Amount required from dollar sources.
[2] Primarily raw materials, such as cotton, wool, nonferrous metals, woodpulp, hides and leather, and chemicals, not covered in the studies of the technical committees; also includes 110 million dollars for semi-manufactures, 1,390 million dollars for consumer goods, and 500 million dollars for ships and airplanes.

TABLE III

Estimated net balance of payments of the participating countries, their dependent territories, and western Germany, 1948–51.
(In millions of United States dollars)

	1948	*1949*	*1950*	*1951*	*Total*
With United States . .	−6,091	−4,532	−3,355	−2,495	−16,473
With other Western Hemisphere . .	−1,944	−1,818	−1,295	−915	−5,972
Total Western Hemisphere	−8,035	−6,350	−4,650	−3,410	−22,445
With rest of world . .	−240	+250	+1,000	+1,800	+2,810
Total–All countries. .	−8,275	−6,100	−3,650	−1,610	−19,635

Note. − indicates deficit; + indicates surplus. Data for 1948 were calculated on the basis of prices ruling on 1 July 1947. Data for 1949–51 were adjusted for estimated changes in the relation between the cost of imports and price of exports and, hence, are not comparable with other statistics. See General Report of the CEEC, vol. I, pp. 121–22.

PLEDGES MADE IN THE REPORT OF THE COMMITTEE OF EUROPEAN ECONOMIC CO-OPERATION

In order to ensure that the recovery program is carried out, the sixteen participating countries pledge themselves to join together, and invite other European countries to join with them, in working to this end. This pledge is undertaken by each country with respect to its own national program, but it also takes into account similar pledges made by the other participating countries. In particular, each country undertakes to use all its efforts—

(i) to develop its production to reach the targets, especially for food and coal;

(ii) to make the fullest and most effective use of its existing productive capacity and all available manpower;

(iii) to modernize its equipment and transport, so that labor becomes more productive, conditions of work are improved, and standards of living of all people of Europe are raised;

(iv) to apply all necessary measures leading to the rapid achievement of internal financial monetary and economic stability while maintaining in each country a high level of employment;

(v) to co-operate with one another and with like-minded countries in all possible steps to reduce the tariffs and other barriers to the expansion of trade both between themselves and with the rest of the world, in accordance with the principles of the draft Charter for an International Trade Organization;

(vi) to remove progressively the obstacles to the free movement of persons within Europe;

(vii) to organize together the means by which common resources can be developed in partnership.

The countries represented on the Committee of Co-operation have pledged themselves that, where stabilization programs are required, they will carry them out in a spirit of determination.

The Governments represented on the Committee of Co-operation have pledged themselves after stabilization has been fully achieved and can be successfully maintained to make their currencies convertible as defined in the Articles of Agreement of the International Monetary Fund at appropriate rates of exchange. The Governments concerned further pledge themselves that any external assistance received for this purpose will be used for this purpose only and applied in constructive and comprehensive measures to put an end to inflation and eventually, when the necessary conditions have been fulfilled, to make their currencies convertible.

To achieve the freer movement of goods, the participating countries are resolved—

(i) to abolish, as soon as possible, the abnormal restrictions which at present hamper their mutual trade;

(ii) to aim, as between themselves and the rest of the world, at a sound and balanced multilateral trading system based on the principles which have guided the framers of the draft Charter for an International Trade Organization.

Arrangements have been made for continuing this work of mutual help and consultation begun in Paris, both through the United Nations machinery and in other ways.

UNDER PETROLEUM PRODUCTS

During the period 1948–51 it is the intention of the participating countries to—

(a) continue efforts to increase production both at home and in dependent oversea territories;

(b) develop oil production in overseas concessions outside the dependent territories;

(c) develop refining capacity at home with a view to economizing in dollar currency, providing raw materials for the increasingly important chemicals from oil industries, and working up at the main centres of consumption the increasing oil output of the Middle East, for which sufficient refining capacity is not at present available.

The participating countries will do all that lies in their power to promote the development of production in their overseas territories, and this will be a further contribution to the narrowing of the gap. Moreover, these countries will do all that lies in their power to develop and make more efficient their production of exportable goods and thus will provide a condition, so far as they are concerned, for a rapid expansion of their exports to the American continent.

SPEECH BY THE RT HON. ERNEST BEVIN, M.P., URGING WESTERN EUROPEAN ECONOMIC CO-OPERATION

(*Extract*)

House of Commons, 22 January 1948

Perhaps I may now return to the subject of the organization in respect of a Western Union. That is its right description. I would emphasize that I am not concerned only with Europe as a geographical conception. Europe has extended its influence throughout the world, and we have to look further afield. In the first place, we turn our eyes to Africa, where great responsibilities are shared by us with South Africa, France, Belgium and Portugal, and equally to all overseas territories, especially of South-East Asia, with which the Dutch are closely concerned. The organization of Western Europe must be economically supported. That involves the closest possible collaboration with the Commonwealth and with overseas territories, not only British but French, Dutch, Belgian, and Portuguese.

These overseas territories are large primary producers, and their standard of life is evolving rapidly and is capable of great development. They have raw materials, food, and resources which can be turned to very great common advantage, both to the people of the territories themselves, to Europe, and to the world as a whole. The other two great world Powers, the United States and Soviet Russia, have tremendous resources. There is no need of conflict with them in this matter at all. If Western Europe is to achieve its balance of payments and to get a world equilibrium, it is essential that those resources should be developed and made available, and the exchange between them carried out in a correct and proper manner. There is no conflict between the social and economic development of those overseas territories to the advantage of their people, and their development as a source of supplies for Western Europe, as a contributor, as I have indicated, so essential to the balance of payments.

What is to be the best method of dealing with this matter? We have been considering and planning for the territories for which we are responsible so as to establish particularly out of our capital production year by year, and also out of our production of consumption goods, a proper proportion in the right order of priorities to assist this development. Coincident with that planning, welfare and cultural development are being pushed ahead with great speed.

C   25

Therefore, if we get the plan, we intend to develop the economic co-operation between Western European countries step by step, to develop the resources of the territories with which we are associated, to build them up a system of priorities which will produce the quickest, most effective and most lasting results for the whole world. We hope that other countries with dependent territories will do the same in association with us.

We shall, thus, bring together resources, manpower, organization and opportunity for millions of people. I would like to depict what it really involves in terms of population whose standard of life can be lifted. We are bringing together these tremendous resources, which stretch through Europe, the Middle East and Africa, to the Far East. In no case would it be an exclusive effort. It would be done with the object of making the whole world richer and safer. We believe there is an opportunity, and that when it is studied there will be a willingness on the part of our friends in the Commonwealth to co-operate with us in this great effort.

BRUSSELS TREATY

TREATY OF ECONOMIC, SOCIAL AND CULTURAL COLLABORATION AND COLLECTIVE SELF-DEFENCE BETWEEN HIS MAJESTY IN RESPECT OF THE UNITED KINGDOM OF GREAT BRITAIN AND NORTHERN IRELAND, HIS ROYAL HIGHNESS THE PRINCE REGENT OF BELGIUM, THE PRESIDENT OF THE FRENCH REPUBLIC, HER ROYAL HIGHNESS THE GRAND DUCHESS OF LUXEMBOURG AND HER MAJESTY THE QUEEN OF THE NETHERLANDS[1]

Brussels, 17 March 1948

Article I

Convinced of the close community of their interests and of the necessity of uniting in order to promote the economic recovery of Europe, the High Contracting Parties will so organize and co-ordinate their economic activities as to produce the best possible results, by the elimination of conflict in their economic policies, the co-ordination of production and the development of commercial exchanges.

The co-operation provided for in the preceding paragraph, which will be effected through the Consultative Council referred to in Article VII as well as through other bodies, shall not involve any duplication of, or prejudice to, the work of other economic organizations in which the High Contracting Parties are or may be represented but shall on the contrary assist the work of those organizations.

Article II

The High Contracting Parties will make every effort in common, both by direct consultation and in specialized agencies, to promote the attainment of a higher standard of living by their peoples and to develop on corresponding lines the social and other related services of their countries.

The High Contracting Parties will consult with the object of achieving the earliest possible application of recommendations of immediate practical interest, relating to social matters, adopted with their approval in the specialized agencies.

[1] Cmd. 7367.

They will endeavour to conclude as soon as possible conventions with each other in the sphere of social security.

Article III

The High Contracting Parties will make every effort in common to lead their peoples towards a better understanding of the principles which form the basis of their common civilization and to promote cultural exchanges by conventions between themselves or by other means.

Article IV

If any of the High Contracting Parties should be the object of an armed attack in Europe, the other High Contracting Parties will, in accordance with the provisions of Article 51 of the Charter of the United Nations, afford the Party so attacked all the military and other aid and assistance in their power.

Article V

All measures taken as a result of the preceding Article shall be immediately reported to the Security Council. They shall be terminated as soon as the Security Council has taken the measures necessary to maintain or restore international peace and security.

The present Treaty does not prejudice in any way the obligations of the High Contracting Parties under the provisions of the Charter of the United Nations. It shall not be interpreted as affecting in any way the authority and responsibility of the Security Council under the Charter to take at any time such action as it deems necessary in order to maintain or restore international peace and security.

Article VI

The High Contracting Parties declare, each so far as he is concerned, that none of the international engagements now in force between him and any other of the High Contracting Parties or any third State is in conflict with the provisions of the present Treaty.

None of the High Contracting Parties will conclude any alliance or participate in any coalition directed against any other of the High Contracting Parties.

Article VII

For the purpose of consulting together on all the questions dealt with in the present Treaty, the High Contracting Parties will create a Consultative Council, which shall be so organized as to be able to exercise its functions continuously. The Council shall meet at such times as it shall deem fit.

At the request of any of the High Contracting Parties, the Council shall be immediately convened in order to permit the High Contracting Parties to consult with regard to any situation which may constitute a threat to peace, in whatever area this threat should arise; with regard to the attitude to be adopted and the steps to be taken in case of a renewal by Germany of an aggressive policy; or with regard to any situation constituting a danger to economic stability.

Article VIII

In pursuance of their determination to settle disputes only by peaceful means, the High Contracting Parties will apply to disputes between themselves the following provisions:

The High Contracting Parties will, while the present Treaty remains in force, settle all disputes falling within the scope of Article 36, paragraph 2, of the Statute of the International Court of Justice[1] by referring them to the Court, subject only, in the case of each of them, to any reservation already made by that Party when accepting this clause for compulsory jurisdiction to the extent that that Party may maintain the reservation.

In addition, the High Contracting Parties will submit to conciliation all disputes outside the scope of Article 36, paragraph 2, of the Statute of the International Court of Justice.

In the case of a mixed dispute involving both questions for which conciliation is appropriate and other questions for which judicial settlement is appropriate, any Party to the dispute shall have the right to insist that the judicial settlement of the legal questions shall precede conciliation.

The preceding provisions of this Article in no way affect the application of relevant provisions or agreements prescribing some other method of pacific settlement.

Article IX

The High Contracting Parties may, by agreement, invite any other State to accede to the present Treaty on conditions to be agreed between them and the State so invited.

Any State so invited may become a Party to the Treaty by depositing an instrument of accession with the Belgian Government.

The Belgian Government will inform each of the High Contracting Parties of the deposit of each instrument of accession.

[1] 'Treaty Series No. 67 (1946),' Cmd. 7015, p. 25.

Article X

The present Treaty shall be ratified and the instruments of ratification shall be deposited as soon as possible with the Belgian Government.

It shall enter into force on the date of the deposit of the last instrument of ratification and shall thereafter remain in force for fifty years.

After the expiry of the period of fifty years, each of the High Contracting Parties shall have the right to cease to be a party thereto provided that he shall have previously given one year's notice of denunciation to the Belgian Government.

The Belgian Government shall inform the Governments of the other High Contracting Parties of the deposit of each instrument of ratification and of each notice of denunciation.

In witness whereof, the above-mentioned Plenipotentiaries have signed the present Treaty and have affixed thereto their seals.

Done at Brussels, this seventeenth day of March 1948, in English and French, each text being equally authentic, in a single copy which shall remain deposited in the archives of the Belgian Government and of which certified copies shall be transmitted by that Government to each of the other signatories.

[*Here follow the Signatures*]

FOREIGN ASSISTANCE ACT[1]

Approved, 3 April 1948

TITLE I

SEC. 101. This title may be cited as the 'Economic Co-operation Act of 1948'.

FINDINGS AND DECLARATION OF POLICY

SEC. 102. (a) Recognizing the intimate economic and other relationships between the United States and the nations of Europe, and recognizing that disruption following in the wake of war is not contained by national frontiers, the Congress finds that the existing situation in Europe endangers the establishment of a lasting peace, the general welfare and national interest of the United States, and the attainment of the objectives of the United Nations. The restoration or maintenance in European countries of principles of individual liberty, free institutions, and genuine independence rests largely upon the establishment of sound economic conditions, stable international economic relationships, and the achievement by the countries of Europe of a healthy economy independent of extraordinary outside assistance. The accomplishment of these objectives calls for a plan of European recovery, open to all such nations which co-operate in such plan, based upon a strong production effort, the expansion of foreign trade, the creation and maintenance of internal financial stability, and the development of economic co-operation, including all possible steps to establish and maintain equitable rates of exchange and to bring about the progressive elimination of trade barriers. Mindful of the advantages which the United States has enjoyed through the existence of a large domestic market with no internal trade barriers, and believing that similar advantages can accrue to the countries of Europe, it is declared to be the policy of the people of the United States to encourage these countries through a joint organization to exert sustained common efforts as set forth in the report of the Committee of European Economic Co-operation signed at Paris on 22 September 1947, which will speedily achieve that economic co-operation in Europe which is essential for lasting peace and prosperity. It is further declared to be the policy of the people of the United States to sustain and strengthen principles of

[1] Public Law 472—80th Congress. Chapter 169—2nd Session. S. 2202.

individual liberty, free institutions, and genuine independence in Europe through assistance to those countries of Europe which participate in a joint recovery program based upon self-help and mutual co-operation: *Provided*, That no assistance to the participating countries herein contemplated shall seriously impair the economic stability of the United States. It is further declared to be the policy of the United States that continuity of assistance provided by the United States should, at all times, be dependent upon continuity of co-operation among countries participating in the program.

PURPOSES OF TITLE

(*b*) It is the purpose of this title to effectuate the policy set forth in subsection (*a*) of this section by furnishing material and financial assistance to the participating countries in such a manner as to aid them, through their own individual and concerted efforts, to become independent of extraordinary outside economic assistance within the period of operations under this title, by—

(1) promoting industrial and agricultural production in the participating countries;

(2) furthering the restoration or maintenance of the soundness of European currencies, budgets, and finances; and

(3) facilitating and stimulating the growth of international trade of participating countries with one another and with other countries by appropriate measures including reduction of barriers which may hamper such trade.

PARTICIPATING COUNTRIES

SEC. 103. (*a*) As used in this title, the term 'participating country' means—

(1) any country, together with dependent areas under its administration, which signed the report of the Committee of European Economic Co-operation at Paris on 22 September 1947; and

(2) any other country (including any of the zones of occupation of Germany, any areas under international administration or control, and the Free Territory of Trieste or either of its zones) wholly or partly in Europe, together with dependent areas under its administration;

provided such country adheres to, and for so long as it remains an adherent to, a joint program for European recovery designed to accomplish the purposes of this title.

(*b*) Until such time as the Free Territory of Trieste or either of its zones becomes eligible for assistance under this title as a partici-

32

pating country, assistance to the Free Territory of Trieste, or either of its zones, is hereby authorized under the Foreign Aid Act of 1947 until 30 June 1949, and the said Foreign Aid Act of 1947 is hereby amended accordingly, and not to exceed $20,000,000 out of funds authorized to be advanced by the Reconstruction Finance Corporation under subsection (a) of Section 114 of this title, or under subsection (d) of Section 11 of the Foreign Aid Act of 1947 notwithstanding any appropriation heretofore made under such Act, may be utilized for the purposes of this subsection: *Provided*, That Section 11 (b) of the Foreign Aid Act of 1947 shall not apply in respect of the Free Territory of Trieste or either of its zones: *And provided further*, That the provisions of Section 115 (b) (6) of this title shall apply to local currency deposited pursuant to Section 5 (b) of that Act.

ESTABLISHMENT OF ECONOMIC CO-OPERATION ADMINISTRATION

SEC. 104. (a) There is hereby established, with its principal office in the District of Columbia, an agency of the Government which shall be known as the Economic Co-operation Administration, hereinafter referred to as the Administration. The Administration shall be headed by an Administrator for Economic Co-operation, hereinafter referred to as the Administrator, who shall be appointed by the President, by and with the advice and consent of the Senate, and who shall receive compensation at the rate of $20,000 per annum. The Administrator shall be responsible to the President and shall have a status in the executive branch of the Government comparable to that of the head of an executive department. Except as otherwise provided in this title, the administration of the provisions of this title is hereby vested in the Administrator and his functions shall be performed under the control of the President.

(b) There shall be in the Administration a Deputy Administrator for Economic Co-operation who shall be appointed by the President, by and with the advice and consent of the Senate, and shall receive compensation at the rate of $17,500 per annum. The Deputy Administrator for Economic Co-operation shall perform such functions as the Administrator shall designate, and shall be Acting Administrator for Economic Co-operation during the absence or disability of the Administrator or in the event of a vacancy in the office of Administrator.

(c) The President is authorized, pending the appointment and qualification of the first Administrator or Deputy Administrator for Economic Co-operation appointed hereunder, to provide, for a period of not to exceed thirty days after the date of enactment of this Act, for the performance of the functions of the Administrator under this title through such departments, agencies, or establishments of the United States Government as he may direct. In the event the President nominates an Administrator or Deputy Administrator prior to the expiration of such thirty-day period, the authority conferred upon the President by this subsection shall be extended beyond such thirty-day period but only until an Administrator or Deputy Administrator qualifies and takes office.

(d) (1) The Administrator, with the approval of the President, is hereby authorized and empowered to create a corporation with such powers as the Administrator may deem necessary or appropriate for the accomplishment of the purposes of this title.

(2) If a corporation is created under this section—

(i) it shall have the power to sue and be sued, to acquire, hold, and dispose of property, to use its revenues, to determine the character of any necessity for its obligations and expenditures and the manner in which they shall be incurred, allowed and paid, and to exercise such other powers as may be necessary or appropriate to carry out the purposes of the corporation;

(ii) its powers shall be set out in a charter which shall be valid only when certified copies thereof are filed with the Secretary of the Senate and the Clerk of the House of Representatives and published in the Federal Register, and all amendments to such charter shall be valid only when similarly filed and published;

(iii) it shall not have succession beyond 30 June 1952, except for purposes of liquidation, unless its life is extended beyond such date pursuant to Act of Congress; and

(iv) it shall be subject to the Government Corporation Control Act to the same extent as wholly owned Government corporations listed in Section 101 of such Act.

(3) All capital stock of the corporation shall be of one class, be issued for cash only, and be subscribed for by the Administrator. Payment for such capital stock shall be made from funds available for the purposes of this title.

(e) Any department, agency, or establishment of the Government (including, whenever used in this title, any corporation which is an instrumentality of the United States) performing functions under this title is authorized to employ, for duty within the continental limits of the United States, such personnel as may be necessary to carry out the provisions and purposes of this title, and funds available pursuant to Section 114 of this title shall be available for personal services in the District of Columbia and elsewhere without regard to Section 14 (a) of the Federal Employees Pay Act of 1946 (60 Stat. 219). Of such personnel employed by the Administration, not to exceed one hundred may be compensated without regard to the provisions of the Classification Act of 1923, as amended, of whom not more than twenty-five may be compensated at a rate in excess of

$10,000 per annum, but not in excess of $15,000 per annum. Experts and consultants or organizations thereof, as authorized by Section 15 of the Act of 2 August 1946 (U. S. C., title 5, sec. 55a), may be employed by the Administration, and individuals so employed may be compensated at rates not in excess of $50 per diem and while away from their homes or regular places of business, they may be paid actual travel expenses and not to exceed $10 per diem in lieu of subsistence and other expenses while so employed.

(*f*) The Administrator may, from time to time, promulgate such rules and regulations as may be necessary and proper to carry out his functions under this title, and he may delegate authority to perform any of such functions to his subordinates, acting under his direction and under rules and regulations promulgated by him.

GENERAL FUNCTIONS OF ADMINISTRATOR

SEC. 105. (*a*) The Administrator, under the control of the President, shall in addition to all other functions vested in him by this title—

(1) review and appraise the requirements of participating countries for assistance under the terms of this title;

(2) formulate programs of United States assistance under this title, including approval of specific projects which have been submitted to him by the participating countries;

(3) provide for the efficient execution of any such programs as may be placed in operation; and

(4) terminate provision of assistance or take other remedial action as provided in Section 118 of this title.

(*b*) In order to strengthen and make more effective the conduct of the foreign relations of the United States—

(1) the Administrator and the Secretary of State shall keep each other fully and currently informed on matters, including prospective action, arising within the scope of their respective duties which are pertinent to the duties of the other;

(2) whenever the Secretary of State believes that any action, proposed action, or failure to act on the part of the Administrator is inconsistent with the foreign-policy objectives of the United States, he shall consult with the Administrator and, if differences of view are not adjusted by consultation, the matter shall be referred to the President for final decision;

(3) whenever the Administrator believes that any action, proposed action, or failure to act on the part of the Secretary of State in performing functions under this title is inconsistent with the purposes and provisions of this title, he shall consult with the

Secretary of State and, if differences of view are not adjusted by consultation, the matter shall be referred to the President for final decision.

(c) The Administrator and the department, agency, or officer in the executive branch of the Government exercising the authority granted to the President by Section 6 of the Act of 2 July 1940 (54 Stat. 714), as amended, shall keep each other fully and currently informed on matters, including prospective action, arising within the scope of their respective duties which are pertinent to the duties of the other. Whenever the Administrator believes that any action, proposed action, or failure to act on the part of such department, agency, or officer in performing functions under this title is inconsistent with the purposes and provisions of this title, he shall consult with such department, agency, or officer and, if differences of view are not adjusted by consultation, the matter shall be referred to the President for final decision.

NATIONAL ADVISORY COUNCIL

SEC. 106. Section 4 (a) of the Bretton Woods Agreements Act (59 Stat. 512, 513) is hereby amended to read as follows:

'SEC. 4. (a) In order to co-ordinate the policies and operations of the representatives of the United States on the Fund and the Bank and of all agencies of the Government which make or participate in making foreign loans or which engage in foreign financial, exchange or monetary transactions, there is hereby established the National Advisory Council on International Monetary and Financial Problems (hereinafter referred to as the "Council"), consisting of the Secretary of the Treasury, as Chairman, the Secretary of State, the Secretary of Commerce, the Chairman of the Board of Governors of the Federal Reserve System, the Chairman of the Board of Directors of the Export-Import Bank of Washington, and during such period as the Economic Co-operation Administration shall continue to exist, the Administrator for Economic Co-operation.'

PUBLIC ADVISORY BOARD

SEC. 107. (a) There is hereby created a Public Advisory Board, hereinafter referred to as the Board, which shall advise and consult with the Administrator with respect to general or basic policy matters arising in connection with the Administrator's discharge of his responsibilities. The Board shall consist of the Administrator, who shall be Chairman, and not to exceed twelve additional members to be appointed by the President, by and with the advice and consent of the Senate, and who shall be selected from among citizens of the United States of broad and varied experience in matters affecting

36

the public interest, other than officers and employees of the United States (including any agency or instrumentality of the United States) who, as such, regularly receive compensation for current services. The Board shall meet at least once a month and at other times upon the call of the Administrator or when three or more members of the Board request the Administrator to call a meeting. Not more than a majority of two of the members shall be appointed to the Board from the same political party. Members of the Board, other than the Administrator, shall receive, out of funds made available for the purposes of this title, a per diem allowance of $50 for each day spent away from their homes or regular places of business, for the purpose of attendance at meetings of the Board, or at conferences held upon the call of the Administrator, and in necessary travel, and while so engaged, they may be paid actual travel expenses and not to exceed $10 per diem in lieu of subsistence and other expenses.

(b) The Administrator may appoint such other advisory committees as he may determine to be necessary or desirable to effectuate the purposes of this title.

UNITED STATES SPECIAL REPRESENTATIVE ABROAD

SEC. 108. There shall be a United States Special Representative in Europe who shall (a) be appointed by the President, by and with the advice and consent of the Senate, (b) be entitled to receive the same compensation and allowances as a chief of mission, class 1, within the meaning of the Act of 13 August 1946 (60 Stat. 999), and (c) have the rank of ambassador extraordinary and plenipotentiary. He shall be the representative of the Administrator, and shall also be the chief representative of the United States Government to any organization of participating countries which may be established by such countries to further a joint program for European recovery, and shall discharge in Europe such additional responsibilities as may be assigned to him with the approval of the President in furtherance of the purposes of this title. He may also be designated as the United States representative on the Economic Commission for Europe. He shall receive his instructions from the Administrator and such instructions shall be prepared and transmitted to him in accordance with procedures agreed to between the Administrator and the Secretary of State in order to assure appropriate co-ordination as provided by subsection (b) of Section 105 of this title. He shall co-ordinate the activities of the chiefs of special missions provided for in Section 109 of this title. He shall keep the Administrator, the Secretary of State, the chiefs of the United States diplomatic missions, and the chiefs of the special missions provided for in Section 109 of this title currently informed concerning his activities. He shall consult with the chiefs of all such missions, who shall give him such co-operation as he may require for the performance of his duties under this title.

SPECIAL ECA MISSIONS ABROAD

SEC. 109. (*a*) There shall be established for each participating country, except as provided in subsection (*d*) of this section, a special mission for economic co-operation under the direction of a chief who shall be responsible for assuring the performance within such country of operations under this title. The chief shall be appointed by the Administrator, shall receive his instructions from the Administrator, and shall report to the Administrator on the performance of the duties assigned to him. The chief of the special mission shall take rank immediately after the chief of the United States diplomatic mission in such country.

(*b*) The chief of the special mission shall keep the chief of the United States diplomatic mission fully and currently informed on matters, including prospective action, arising within the scope of the operations of the special mission and the chief of the diplomatic mission shall keep the chief of the special mission fully and currently informed on matters relative to the conduct of the duties of the chief of the special mission. The chief of the United States diplomatic mission will be responsible for assuring that the operations of the special mission are consistent with the foreign-policy objectives of the United States in such country and to that end whenever the chief of the United States diplomatic mission believes that any action, proposed action, or failure to act on the part of the special mission is inconsistent with such foreign-policy objectives, he shall so advise the chief of the special mission and the United States Special Representative in Europe. If differences of view are not adjusted by consultation, the matter shall be referred to the Secretary of State and the Administrator for decision.

(*c*) The Secretary of State shall provide such office space, facilities, and other administrative services for the United States Special Representative in Europe and his staff, and for the special mission in each participating country, as may be agreed between the Secretary of State and the Administrator.

(*d*) With respect to any of the zones of occupation of Germany and of the Free Territory of Trieste, during the period of occupation, the President shall make appropriate administrative arrangements for the conduct of operations under this title, in order to enable the Administrator to carry out his responsibility to assure the accomplishment of the purposes of this title.

38

PERSONNEL OUTSIDE UNITED STATES

SEC. 110. (*a*) For the purpose of performing functions under this title outside the continental limits of the United States the Administrator may—

(1) employ persons who shall receive compensation at any of the rates provided for the Foreign Service Reserve and Staff by the Foreign Service Act of 1946 (60 Stat. 999), together with allowances and benefits established thereunder; and

(2) recommend the appointment or assignment of persons, and the Secretary of State may appoint or assign such persons, to any class in the Foreign Service Reserve or Staff for the duration of operations under this title, and the Secretary of State may assign, transfer, or promote such persons upon the recommendation of the Administrator. Persons so appointed to the Foreign Service Staff shall be entitled to the benefits of Section 528 of the Foreign Service Act of 1946.

(*b*) For the purpose of performing functions under this title outside the continental limits of the United States, the Secretary of State may, at the request of the Administrator, appoint, for the duration of operations under this title, alien clerks and employees in accordance with applicable provisions of the Foreign Service Act of 1946 (60 Stat. 999).

(*c*) No citizen or resident of the United States may be employed, or if already employed, may be assigned to duties by the Secretary of State or the Administrator under this title for a period to exceed three months unless such individual has been investigated as to loyalty and security by the Federal Bureau of Investigation and a report thereon has been made to the Secretary of State and the Administrator, and until the Secretary of State or the Administrator has certified in writing (and filed copies thereof with the Senate Committee on Foreign Relations and the House Committee on Foreign Affairs) that, after full consideration of such report, he believes such individual is loyal to the United States, its Constitution, and form of government, and is not now and has never been a member of any organization advocating contrary views. This subsection shall not apply in the case of any officer appointed by the President by and with the advice and consent of the Senate.

NATURE AND METHOD OF ASSISTANCE

SEC. 111. (*a*) The Administrator may, from time to time, furnish assistance to any participating country by providing for the performance of any of the functions set forth in paragraphs (1) through (5) of this subsection when he deems it to be in furtherance of the purposes of this title, and upon the terms and conditions set forth in this title and such additional terms and conditions consistent with the provisions of this title as he may determine to be necessary and proper.

(1) Procurement from any source, including Government stocks on the same basis as procurement by Government agencies under Public Law 375 (Seventy-ninth Congress) for their own use, of any commodity which he determines to be required for the furtherance of the purposes of this title. As used in this title, the term 'commodity' means any commodity, material, article, supply, or goods necessary for the purposes of this title.

(2) Processing, storing, transporting, and repairing any commodities, or performing any other services with respect to a participating country which he determines to be required for accomplishing the purposes of this title. The Administrator shall, in providing for the procurement of commodities under authority of this title, take such steps as may be necessary to assure, so far as is practicable, that at least 50 per centum of the gross tonnage of commodities, procured within the United States out of funds made available under this title and transported abroad on ocean vessels, is so transported on United States flag vessels to the extent such vessels are available at market rates.

(3) Procurement of and furnishing technical information and assistance.

(4) Transfer of any commodity or service, which transfer shall be signified by delivery of the custody and right of possession and use of such commodity, or otherwise making available any such commodity, or by rendering a service to a participating country or to any agency or organization representing a participating country.

(5) The allocation of commodities or services to specific projects designed to carry out the purposes of this title, which have been submitted to the Administrator by participating countries and have been approved by him.

(b) In order to facilitate and maximize the use of private channels of trade, subject to adequate safeguards to assure that all expenditures in connection with such procurement are within approved programs in accordance with terms and conditions established by the Administrator, he may provide for the performance of any of the functions described in subsection (a) of this section—

(1) by establishing accounts against which, under regulations prescribed by the Administrator—

(i) letters of commitment may be issued in connection with supply programs approved by the Administrator (and such letters of commitment, when issued, shall constitute obligations of the United States and monies due or to become due thereunder shall be assignable under the Assignment of Claims Act of 1940 and shall constitute obligations of applicable appropriations); and

(ii) withdrawals may be made by participating countries, or agencies or organizations representing participating countries or by other persons or organizations, upon presentation of contracts, invoices, or other documentation specified by the Administrator under arrangements prescribed by the Administrator to assure the use of such withdrawals for purposes approved by the Administrator.

Such accounts may be established on the books of the Administration, or any other department, agency, or establishment of the Government specified by the Administrator, or, on terms and conditions approved by the Secretary of the Treasury, in banking institutions in the United States. Expenditures of funds which have been made available through accounts so established shall be accounted for on standard documentation required for expenditures of Government funds: *Provided*, That such expenditures for commodities or services procured outside the continental limits of the United States under authority of this section may be accounted for exclusively on such certification as the Administrator may prescribe in regulations promulgated by him with the approval of the Comptroller General of the United States to assure expenditure in furtherance of the purposes of this title.

(2) by utilizing the services and facilities of any department, agency, or establishment of the Government as the President shall direct, or with the consent of the head of such department, agency, or establishment, or, in the President's discretion, by acting in co-operation with the United Nations or with other international organizations or with agencies of the participating countries, and funds allocated pursuant to this section to any department, agency, or establishment of the Government shall be established in separate appropriation accounts on the books of the Treasury.

(3) by making, under rules and regulations to be prescribed by the Administrator, guaranties to any person of investments in connection with projects approved by the Administrator and the participating country concerned as furthering the purposes of this title (including guaranties of investments in enterprises producing or distributing informational media: *Provided*, That the amount of such guaranties in the first year after the date of the enactment of this Act does not exceed $15,000,000), which guaranties shall terminate not later than fourteen years from the date of enactment of this Act: *Provided*, That—

(i) the guaranty to any person shall not exceed the amount of dollars invested in the project by such person with the approval of the Administrator and shall be limited to the transfer into United States dollars of other currencies, or credits in such currencies, received by such person as income from the approved investment, as repayment or return thereof, in whole or in part, or as compensation for the sale or disposition of all or any part thereof: *Provided*, That, when any payment is made to any person under authority of this paragraph, such currencies, or credits in such currencies, shall become the property of the United States Government;

(ii) the Administrator may charge a fee in an amount determined by him not exceeding 1 per centum per annum of the amount of each guaranty, and all fees collected hereunder shall be available for expenditure in discharge of liabilities under guaranties made under this paragraph until such time as all such liabilities have been discharged or have expired, or until all such fees have been expended in accordance with the provisions of this paragraph; and

(iii) as used in this paragraph, the term 'person' means a citizen of the United States or any corporation, partnership, or other association created under the law of the United States or of any State or Territory and substantially beneficially owned by citizens of the United States.

The total amount of the guaranties made under this paragraph (3) shall not exceed $300,000,000, and as such guaranties are made the authority to realize funds from the sale of notes for the purpose of allocating funds to the Export-Import Bank of Washington under paragraph (2) of subsection (c) of this section shall be accordingly reduced. Any payments made to discharge liabilities under guaranties issued under paragraph (3) of this subsection shall be paid out of fees collected under subparagraph (ii) of paragraph (3) of this subsection as long as such fees are available, and thereafter shall be paid out of funds realized from the sale of notes which shall be issued under authority of paragraph (2) of subsection (c) of this section when necessary to discharge liabilities under any such guaranty.

(c) (1) The Administrator may provide assistance for any participating country, in the form and under the procedures authorized in subsections (a) and (b), respectively, of this section, through grants or upon payment in cash, or on credit terms, or on such other terms of payment as he may find appropriate, including payment by the transfer to the United States (under such terms and in such quantities as may be agreed to between the Administrator and the participating country) of materials which are required by the United States as a result of deficiencies or potential deficiencies in its own resources. In determining whether such assistance shall be through grants or upon terms of payment, and in determining the terms of payment, he shall act in consultation with the National Advisory Council on International Monetary and Financial Problems, and the determination whether or not a participating country should be required to make payment for any assistance furnished to such country in furtherance of the purposes of this title, and the terms of such payment, if required, shall depend upon the character and purpose of the assistance and upon whether there is reasonable assurance of repayment considering the capacity of such country to make such payments without jeopardizing the accomplishment of the purposes of this title.

(2) When it is determined that assistance should be extended under the provisions of this title on credit terms, the Administrator shall allocate funds for the purpose to the Export-Import Bank of Washington, which shall, notwithstanding the provisions of the Export-Import Bank Act of 1945 (59 Stat. 526), as amended, make and administer the credit on terms specified by the Administrator in consultation with the National Advisory Council on International Monetary and Financial Problems. The Administrator is authorized to issue notes from time to time for purchase by the Secretary of the Treasury in an amount not exceeding in the aggregate $1,000,000,000 (i) for the purpose of allocating funds to the Export-Import Bank of Washington under this paragraph during the period of one year following the date of enactment of this Act and (ii) for the purpose of carrying out the provisions of paragraph (3) of subsection (b) of this section until all liabilities arising under guaranties made pursuant to such paragraph (3) have expired or have been discharged. Such notes shall be redeemable at the option of the Administrator before maturity in such manner as may be stipulated in such notes and shall have such maturity as may be determined by the Administrator with the approval of the Secretary of the Treasury. Each such note shall bear interest at a rate determined by the Secretary of the Treasury, taking into consideration the current average rate on outstanding marketable obligations of the United States as of the last day of the month preceding the issuance of the note. Payment under this paragraph of the purchase price of such notes and repayments thereof by the Administrator shall be treated as public-debt transactions of the United States. In allocating funds to the Export-Import Bank of Washington under this paragraph, the Administrator shall first utilize such funds realized from the sale of notes authorized by this paragraph as he determines to be available for this purpose, and when such funds are exhausted, or after the end of one year from the date of enactment of this Act, whichever is

43

earlier, he shall utilize any funds appropriated under this title. The Administrator shall make advances to, or reimburse, the Export-Import Bank of Washington for necessary administrative expenses in connection with such credits. Credits made by the Export-Import Bank of Washington with funds so allocated to it by the Administrator shall not be considered in determining whether the Bank has outstanding at any one time loans and guaranties to the extent of the limitation imposed by Section 7 of the Export-Import Bank Act of 1945 (59 Stat. 529), as amended. Amounts received in repayment of principal and interest on any credits made under this paragraph shall be deposited into miscellaneous receipts of the Treasury: *Provided*, That, to the extent required for such purpose, amounts received in repayment of principal and interest on any credits made out of funds realized from the sale of notes authorized under this paragraph shall be deposited into the Treasury for the purpose of the retirement of such notes.

PROTECTION OF DOMESTIC ECONOMY

SEC. 112. (*a*) The Administrator shall provide for the procurement in the United States of commodities under this title in such a way as to (1) minimize the drain upon the resources of the United States and the impact of such procurement upon the domestic economy, and (2) avoid impairing the fulfilment of vital needs of the people of the United States.

(*b*) The procurement of petroleum and petroleum products under this title shall, to the maximum extent practicable, be made from petroleum sources outside the United States; and, in furnishing commodities under the provisions of this title, the Administrator shall take fully into account the present and anticipated world shortage of petroleum and its products and the consequent undesirability of expansion in petroleum-consuming equipment where the use of alternate fuels or other sources of power is practicable.

(*c*) In order to assure the conservation of domestic grain supplies and the retention in the United States of by-product feeds necessary to the maintenance of the agricultural economy of the United States, the amounts of wheat and wheat flour produced in the United States to be transferred by grant to the participating countries shall be so determined that the total quantity of United States wheat used to produce the wheat flour procured in the United States for transfer by grant to such countries under this title shall not be less than 25 per centum of the aggregate of the unprocessed wheat and wheat in the form of flour procured in the United States for transfer by grant to such countries under this title.

(*d*) The term 'surplus agricultural commodity' as used in this

44

section is defined as any agricultural commodity, or product thereof, produced in the United States which is determined by the Secretary of Agriculture to be in excess of domestic requirements. In providing for the procurement of any such surplus agricultural commodity for transfer by grant to any participating country in accordance with the requirements of such country, the Administrator shall, insofar as practicable and where in furtherance of the purposes of this title, give effect to the following:

(1) The Administrator shall authorize the procurement of any such surplus agricultural commodity only within the United States: *Provided*, That this restriction shall not be applicable (i) to any agricultural commodity, or product thereof, located in one participating country, and intended for transfer to another participating country, if the Administrator, in consultation with the Secretary of Agriculture, determines that such procurement and transfer is in furtherance of the purposes of this title, and would not create a burdensome surplus in the United States or seriously prejudice the position of domestic producers of such surplus agricultural commodities, or (ii) if, and to the extent that any such surplus agricultural commodity is not available in the United States in sufficient quantities to supply the requirements of the participating countries under this title.

(2) In providing for the procurement of any such surplus agricultural commodity, the Administrator shall, insofar as practicable and applicable, and after giving due consideration to the excess of any such commodity over domestic requirements, and to the historic reliance of United States producers of any such surplus agricultural commodity upon markets in the participating countries, provide for the procurement of each class or type of any such surplus agricultural commodity in the approximate proportion that the Secretary of Agriculture determines such classes or types bear to the total amount of excess of such surplus agricultural commodity over domestic requirements.

(e) Whenever the Secretary of Agriculture determines that any quantity of any surplus agricultural commodity, heretofore or hereafter acquired by Commodity Credit Corporation in the administration of its price-support programs, is available for use in furnishing assistance to foreign countries, he shall so advise all departments, agencies, and establishments of the Government administering laws providing for the furnishing of assistance or relief to foreign countries (including occupied or liberated countries or areas of such countries). Thereafter the department, agency, or establishment administering any such law shall, to the maximum extent practicable, consistent with the provisions and in furtherance of the purposes of such law, and where for transfer by grant and in accordance with the requirements of such foreign country, procure or provide for the procurement of such quantity of such surplus agricultural commodity. The sales price paid as reimbursement to Commodity Credit Corporation for any such surplus agricultural commodity shall be in such amount as Commodity Credit Corporation determines will fully reimburse it for the cost to it of such surplus agricultural commodity at the time and place such surplus agricultural commodity is delivered by it, but in no event shall the sales price be higher than the domestic market price at such time and place of delivery as determined by the Secretary of Agriculture, and the Secretary of Agriculture may pay not to exceed 50 per centum of such sales price as authorized by subsection (f) of this section.

(f) Subject to the provisions of this section, but notwithstanding any other provision of law, in order to encourage utilization of surplus agricultural commodities pursuant to this or any other Act providing for assistance or relief to foreign countries, the Secretary of Agriculture, in carrying out the purposes of clause (1), Section 32, Public Law 320, Seventy-fourth Congress, as amended, may make payments, including payments to any government agency procuring or selling such surplus agricultural commodities, in an amount not to exceed 50 per centum of the sales price (basis free along ship or free on board vessel, United States ports), as determined by the Secretary of Agriculture, of such surplus agricultural commodities. The rescission of the remainder of Section 32 funds by the Act of 30 July 1947 (Public Law 266, Eightieth Congress), is hereby cancelled and such funds are hereby made available for the purposes of Section 32 for the fiscal year ending 30 June 1948.

(g) No export shall be authorized pursuant to authority conferred by Section 6 of the Act of 2 July 1940 (54 Stat. 714), including any amendment thereto, of any commodity from the United States to any country wholly or partly in Europe which is not a participating country, if the department, agency, or officer in the executive branch of the Government exercising the authority granted to the President by Section 6 of the Act of 2 July 1940, as amended, determines that the supply of such commodity is insufficient (or would be insufficient if such export were permitted) to fulfil the requirements of participating countries under this title as determined by the Administrator: *Provided, however,* That such export may be authorized if such department, agency, or officer determines that such export is otherwise in the national interest of the United States.

(h) In providing for the performance of any of the functions described in subsection (a) of Section 111, the Administrator shall, to the maximum extent consistent with the accomplishment of the purposes of this title, utilize private channels of trade.

REIMBURSEMENT TO GOVERNMENT AGENCIES

SEC. 113. (a) The Administrator shall make reimbursement or payment, out of funds available for the purposes of this title, for any commodity, service, or facility procured under Section 111 of this title from any department, agency, or establishment of the Government. Such reimbursement or payment shall be made to the owning or disposal agency, as the case may be, at replacement cost, or, if required by law, at actual cost, or at any other price authorized by law and agreed to between the Administrator and such agency. The amount of any reimbursement or payment to an owning agency for commodities, services, or facilities so procured shall be credited to current applicable appropriations, funds, or accounts from which there may be procured replacements of similar commodities or such services or facilities: *Provided*, That such commodities, services, or facilities may be procured from an owning agency only with the consent of such agency: *And provided further*, That where such appropriations, funds, or accounts are not reimbursable except by reason of this subsection, and when the owning agency determines that replacement of any commodity procured under authority of this section is not necessary, any funds received in payment therefor shall be covered into the Treasury as miscellaneous receipts.

(b) The Administrator, whenever in his judgement the interests of the United States will best be served thereby, may dispose of any commodity procured out of funds made available for the purposes of this title, in lieu of transferring such commodity to a participating country, (1) by transfer of such commodity, upon reimbursement, to any department, agency, or establishment of the Government for use of disposal by such department, agency, or establishment as authorized by law, or (2) without regard to provisions of law relating to the disposal of Government-owned property, when necessary to prevent spoilage or wastage of such commodity or to conserve the usefulness thereof. Funds realized from such disposal or transfer shall revert to the respective appropriation or appropriations out of which funds were expended for the procurement of such commodity.

AUTHORIZATION OF APPROPRIATIONS

SEC. 114. (a) Notwithstanding the provisions of any other law, the Reconstruction Finance Corporation is authorized and directed, until such time as an appropriation shall be made pursuant to subsection (c) of this section, to make advances not to exceed in the aggregate $1,000,000,000 to carry out the provisions of this title, in such manner, at such time, and in such amounts as the President shall determine, and no interest shall be charged on advances made by the Treasury to the Reconstruction Finance Corporation for this purpose. The Reconstruction Finance Corporation shall be repaid without interest for advances made by it hereunder, from funds made available for the purposes of this title.

(b) Such part as the President may determine of the unobligated and unexpended balances of appropriations or other funds available for the purposes of the Foreign Aid Act of 1947 shall be available for the purpose of carrying out the purposes of this title.

(c) In order to carry out the provisions of this title with respect to those participating countries which adhere to the purposes of this title, and remain eligible to receive assistance hereunder, such funds shall be available as are hereafter authorized and appropriated to the President from time to time through 30 June 1952, to carry out the provisions and accomplish the purposes of this title: *Provided, however,* That for carrying out the provisions and accomplishing the purposes of this title for the period of one year following the date of enactment of this Act, there are hereby authorized to be so appropriated not to exceed $4,300,000,000. Nothing in this title is intended nor shall it be construed as an express or implied commitment to provide any specific assistance, whether of funds, commodities, or services, to any country or countries. The authorization in this title is limited to the period of twelve months in order that subsequent Congresses may pass on any subsequent authorizations.

(d) Funds made available for the purposes of this title shall be available for incurring and defraying all necessary expenses incident to carrying out the provisions of this title, including administrative expenses and expenses for compensation, allowances and travel of personnel, including Foreign Service personnel whose services are utilized primarily for the purposes of this title, and, without regard to the provisions of any other law, for printing and binding, and for expenditures outside the continental limits of the United States for the procurement of supplies and services and for other administrative purposes (other than compensation of personnel) without regard to such laws and regulations governing the obligation and expenditure of government funds, as the Administrator shall specify in the interest of the accomplishment of the purposes of this title.

(e) The unencumbered portions of any deposits which may have been made by any participating country pursuant to Section 6 of the joint resolution providing for relief assistance to the people of countries devastated by war (Public Law 84, Eightieth Congress) and Section 5 (b) of the Foreign Aid Act of 1947 (Public Law 389, Eightieth Congress) may be merged with the deposits to be made by such participating country in accordance with Section 115 (b) (6) of this title, and shall be held or used under the same terms and conditions as are provided in Section 115 (b) (6) of this title.

48

(f) In order to reserve some part of the surplus of the fiscal year 1948 for payments thereafter to be made under this title, there is hereby created on the books of the Treasury of the United States a trust fund to be known as the Foreign Economic Co-operation Trust Fund. Notwithstanding any other provision of law, an amount of $3,000,000,000, out of sums appropriated pursuant to the authorization contained in this title shall, when appropriated, be transferred immediately to the trust fund, and shall thereupon be considered as expended during the fiscal year 1948, for the purpose of reporting governmental expenditures. The Secretary of the Treasury shall be the sole trustee of the trust fund and is authorized and directed to pay out of the fund such amounts as the Administrator shall duly requisition. The first expenditures made out of the appropriations authorized under this title in the fiscal year 1949 shall be made with funds requisitioned by the Administrator out of the trust fund until the fund is exhausted, at which time such fund shall cease to exist. The provisions of this subsection shall not be construed as affecting the application of any provision of law which would otherwise govern the obligation of funds so appropriated or the auditing or submission of accounts of transactions with respect to such funds.

BILATERAL AND MULTILATERAL UNDERTAKINGS

SEC. 115. (a) The Secretary of State, after consultation with the Administrator, is authorized to conclude, with individual participating countries or any number of such countries or with an organization representing any such countries, agreements in furtherance of the purposes of this title. The Secretary of State, before an Administrator or Deputy Administrator shall have qualified and taken office, is authorized to negotiate and conclude such temporary agreements in implementation of subsection (b) of this section as he may deem necessary in furtherance of the purposes of this title: *Provided*, That when an Administrator or Deputy Administrator shall have qualified and taken office, the Secretary of State shall conclude the basic agreements required by subsection (b) of this section only after consultation with the Administrator or Deputy Administrator, as the case may be.

(b) The provision of assistance under this title results from the multilateral pledges of the participating countries to use all their efforts to accomplish a joint recovery program based upon self-help and mutual co-operation as embodied in the report of the Committee of European Economic Co-operation signed at Paris on 22 September 1947, and is contingent upon continuous effort of the participating countries to accomplish a joint recovery program through multilateral undertakings and the establishment of a continuing organization for this purpose. In addition to continued mutual co-operation of the participating countries in such a program, each such country shall conclude an agreement with the United States in order for such country to be eligible to receive assistance under this title. Such agreement shall provide for the adherence of such country to the purposes of this title and shall, where applicable, make appropriate provision, among others, for—

(1) promoting industrial and agricultural production in order to enable the participating country to become independent of extraordinary outside economic assistance; and submitting for the approval of the Administrator, upon his request and whenever he deems it in furtherance of the purposes of this title, specific projects proposed by such country to be undertaken in substantial part with assistance furnished under this title, which projects, whenever practicable, shall include projects for increased production of coal, steel, transportation facilities, and food;

(2) taking financial and monetary measures necessary to stabilize its currency, establish or maintain a valid rate of exchange, to balance its governmental budget as soon as practicable, and generally to restore or maintain confidence in its monetary system;

(3) co-operating with other participating countries in facilitating and stimulating an increasing interchange of goods and services among the participating countries and with other countries and co-operating to reduce barriers to trade among themselves and with other countries;

(4) making efficient and practical use, within the framework of a joint program for European recovery, of the resources of such participating country, including any commodities, facilities, or services furnished under this title, which use shall include, to the extent practicable, taking measures to locate and identify and put into appropriate use, in furtherance of such program, assets, and earnings therefrom, which belong to the citizens of such country and which are situated within the United States, its Territories and possessions;

(5) facilitating the transfer to the United States by sale, exchange, barter, or otherwise for stock-piling or other purposes, for such period of time as may be agreed to and upon reasonable terms and in reasonable quantities, of materials which are required by the United States as a result of deficiencies or potential deficiencies in its own resources, and which may be available in such participating country after due regard for reasonable requirements for domestic use and commercial export of such country;

(6) placing in a special account a deposit in the currency of such country, in commensurate amounts and under such terms

and conditions as may be agreed to between such country and the Government of the United States, when any commodity or service is made available through any means authorized under this title, and is furnished to the participating country on a grant basis. Such special account, together with the unencumbered portions of any deposits which may have been made by such country pursuant to Section 6 of the joint resolution providing for relief assistance to the people of countries devastated by war (Public Law 84, Eightieth Congress) and Section 5 (*b*) of the Foreign Aid Act of 1947 (Public Law 389, Eightieth Congress), shall be held or used within such country for such purposes as may be agreed to between such country and the Administrator in consultation with the National Advisory Council on International Monetary and Financial Problems, and the Public Advisory Board provided for in Section 107 (*a*) for purposes of internal monetary and financial stabilization, for the stimulation of productive activity and the exploration for and development of new sources of wealth, or for such other expenditures as may be consistent with the purposes of this title, including local currency administrative expenditures of the United States incident to operations under this title, and under agreement that any unencumbered balance remaining in such account on 30 June 1952, shall be disposed of within such country for such purposes as may, subject to approval by Act or joint resolution of the Congress, be agreed to between such country and the Government of the United States;

(7) publishing in such country and transmitting to the United States, not less frequently than every calendar quarter after the date of the agreement, full statements of operations under the agreement, including a report of the use of funds, commodities, and services received under this title;

(8) furnishing promptly, upon request of the United States, any relevant information which would be of assistance to the United States in determining the nature and scope of operations and the use of assistance provided under this title;

(9) recognizing the principle of equity in respect to the drain upon the natural resources of the United States and of the recipient countries, by agreeing to negotiate (*a*) a future schedule of minimum availabilities to the United States for future purchase and delivery of a fair share of materials which are required by the United States as a result of deficiencies or potential deficiencies in its own resources at world market prices so as to protect the access of United States industry to an equitable share of such materials either in percentages of production or in absolute quantities from the participating countries, and (*b*) suitable protection for the

right of access for any person as defined in paragraph (iii) of subparagraph (3) of Section 111 (b) in the development of such materials on terms of treatment equivalent to those afforded to the nationals of the country concerned, and (c) an agreed schedule of increased production of such materials where practicable in such participating countries and for delivery of an agreed percentage of such increased production to be transferred to the United States on a long-term basis in consideration of assistance furnished by the Administrator to such countries under this title; and

(10) submitting for the decision of the International Court of Justice or of any arbitral tribunal mutually agreed upon any case espoused by the United States Government involving compensation of a national of the United States for governmental measures affecting his property rights, including contracts with or concessions from such country.

(c) Notwithstanding the provisions of subsection (b) of this section, the Administrator, during the three months after the date of enactment of this Act, may perform with respect to any participating country any of the functions authorized under this title which he may determine to be essential in furtherance of the purposes of this title, if (1) such country has signified its adherence to the purposes of this title and its intention to conclude an agreement pursuant to subsection (b) of this section, and (2) he finds that such country is complying with the applicable provisions of subsection (b) of this section: *Provided*, That, notwithstanding the provisions of this subsection, the Administrator may, through 30 June 1948, provide for the transfer of food, medical supplies, fibers, fuel, petroleum and petroleum products, fertilizer, pesticides, and seed to any country of Europe which participated in the Committee of European Economic Co-operation and which undertook pledges to the other participants therein, when the Administrator determines that the transfer of any such supplies to any such country is essential in order to make it possible to carry out the purposes of this title by alleviating conditions of hunger and cold and by preventing serious economic retrogression.

(d) The Administrator shall encourage the joint organization of the participating countries referred to in subsection (b) of this section to ensure that each participating country makes efficient use of the resources of such country, including any commodities, facilities, or services furnished under this title, by observing and reviewing such use through an effective follow-up system approved by the joint organization.

(e) The Administrator shall encourage arrangements among the participating countries in conjunction with the International Refugee Organization looking toward the largest practicable utilization of

manpower available in any of the participating countries in furtherance of the accomplishment of the purposes of this title.

(*f*) The Administrator will request the Secretary of State to obtain
the agreement of those countries concerned that such capital equipment as is scheduled for removal as reparations from the three
western zones of Germany be retained in Germany if such retention
will most effectively serve the purposes of the European recovery
program.

(*g*) It is the understanding of the Congress that, in accordance
with agreements now in effect, prisoners of war remaining in participating countries shall, if they so freely elect, be repatriated prior to
1 January 1949.

WESTERN HEMISPHERE COUNTRIES

SEC. 116. The President shall take appropriate steps to encourage
all countries in the Western Hemisphere to make available to participating countries such assistance as they may be able to furnish.

OTHER DUTIES OF THE ADMINISTRATOR

SEC. 117. (*a*) The Administrator, in furtherance of the purposes
of Section 115 (*b*) (5), and in agreement with a participating country, shall, whenever practicable, promote, by means of funds made
available for the purposes of this title, an increase in the production
in such participating country of materials which are required by the
United States as a result of deficiencies or potential deficiencies in
the resources within the United States.

(*b*) The Administrator, in co-operation with the Secretary of
Commerce, shall facilitate and encourage, through private and
public travel, transport, and other agencies, the promotion and
development of travel by citizens of the United States to and within
participating countries.

(*c*) In order to further the efficient use of United States voluntary
contributions for relief in participating countries receiving assistance
under this title in the form of grants or any of the zones of occupation
of Germany for which assistance is provided under this title and the
Free Territory of Trieste or either of its zones, funds made available
for the purposes of this title shall be used insofar as practicable by the
Administrator, under rules and regulations prescribed by him, to
pay ocean freight charges from a United States port to a designated
foreign port of entry (1) of supplies donated to, or purchased by,
United States voluntary non-profit relief agencies registered with and
recommended by the Advisory Committee on Voluntary Foreign
Aid for operations in Europe, or (2) of relief packages conforming to

such specified size, weight, and contents, as the Administrator may prescribe originating in the United States and consigned to an individual residing in a participating country receiving assistance under this title in the form of grants or any of the zones of occupation of Germany for which assistance is provided under this title and the Free Territory of Trieste or either of its zones. Where practicable the Administrator is directed to make an agreement with such country for the use of a portion of the deposit of local currency placed in a special account pursuant to paragraph 6 of subsection (b) of Section 115 of this title, for the purpose of defraying the transportation cost of such supplies and relief packages from the port of entry of such country to the designated shipping point of consignee. The Secretary of State, after consultation with the Administrator, shall make agreements where practicable with the participating countries for the free entry of such supplies and relief packages.

(d) The Administrator is directed to refuse delivery insofar as practicable to participating countries of commodities which go into the production of any commodity for delivery to any non-participating European country which commodity would be refused export licences to those countries by the United States in the interest of national security. Whenever the Administrator believes that the issuance of a licence for the export of any commodity to any country wholly or partly in Europe which is not a participating country is inconsistent with the purposes and provisions of this title, he shall so advise the department, agency, or officer in the executive branch of the Government exercising the authority with respect to such commodity granted to the President by Section 6 of the Act of 2 July 1940 (54 Stat. 714), as amended, and, if differences of view are not adjusted by consultation, the matter shall be referred to the President for final decision.

TERMINATION OF ASSISTANCE

Sec. 118. The Administrator, in determining the form and measure of assistance provided under this title to any participating country, shall take into account the extent to which such country is complying with its undertakings embodied in its pledges to other participating countries and in its agreement concluded with the United States under Section 115. The Administrator shall terminate the provision of assistance under this title to any participating country whenever he determines that (1) such country is not adhering to its agreement concluded under Section 115, or is diverting from the purposes of this title assistance provided hereunder, and that in the circumstances remedial action other than termination will not more effectively promote the purposes of this title or (2) because of changed conditions, assistance is no longer consistent with the national interest of the United States. Termination of assistance to any country under this section shall include the termination of deliveries of all supplies scheduled under the aid program for such country and not yet delivered.

EXEMPTION FROM CONTRACT AND ACCOUNTING LAWS

Sec. 119. When the President determines it to be in furtherance of the purposes of this title, the functions authorized under this title may be performed without regard to such provisions of law regulating the making, performance, amendment, or modification of contracts and the expenditure of Government funds as the President may specify.

EXEMPTION FROM CERTAIN FEDERAL LAWS RELATING TO EMPLOYMENT

Sec. 120. Service of an individual as a member of the Public Advisory Board (other than the Administrator) created by section 107 (a), as a member of an advisory committee appointed pursuant to Section 107 (b), as an expert or consultant under Section 104 (e), or as an expert, consultant, or technician under Section 124 (d), shall not be considered as service or employment bringing such individual within the provisions of Section 109 or 113 of the Criminal Code (U. S. C., title 18, secs. 198 and 203), of Section 190 of the Revised Statutes (U. S. C., title 5, sec. 99), or of Section 19 (e) of the Contract Settlement Act of 1944, or of any other Federal law imposing restrictions, requirements, or penalties in relation to the employment of persons, the performance of services, or the payment or receipt of compensation in connection with any claim, proceeding, or matter involving the United States.

UNITED NATIONS

Sec. 121. (a) The President is authorized to request the co-operation of or the use of the services and facilities of the United Nations, its organs and specialized agencies, or other international organizations, in carrying out the purposes of this title, and may make payments, by advancements or reimbursements, for such purposes, out of funds made available for the purposes of this title, as may be necessary therefor, to the extent that special compensation is usually required for such services and facilities. Nothing in this title shall be construed to authorize the Administrator to delegate to or otherwise confer upon any international or foreign organization or agency any of his authority to decide the method of furnishing assistance under this title to any participating country or the amount thereof.

(b) The President shall cause to be transmitted to the Secretary

55

General of the United Nations copies of reports to Congress on the operations conducted under this title.

(c) Any agreements concluded between the United States and participating countries, or groups of such countries, in implementation of the purposes of this title, shall be registered with the United Nations if such registration is required by the Charter of the United Nations.

TERMINATION OF PROGRAM

SEC. 122. (a) After 30 June 1952, or after the date of the passage of a concurrent resolution by the two Houses of Congress before such date, which declares that the powers conferred on the Administrator by or pursuant to subsection (a) of Section 111 of this title are no longer necessary for the accomplishment of the purposes of this title, whichever shall first occur, none of the functions authorized under such provisions may be exercised; except that during the twelve months following such date commodities and services with respect to which the Administrator had, prior to such date, authorized procurement for, shipment to, or delivery in a participating country, may be transferred to such country, and funds appropriated under authority of this title may be obligated during such twelve-month period for the necessary expenses of procurement, shipment, delivery, and other activities essential to such transfer, and shall remain available during such period for the necessary expenses of liquidating operations under this title.

(b) At such time as the President shall find appropriate after such date, and prior to the expiration of the twelve months following such date, the powers, duties, and authority of the Administrator under this title may be transferred to such other departments, agencies, or establishments of the Government as the President shall specify, and the relevant funds, records, and personnel of the Administration may be transferred to the departments, agencies, or establishments to which the related functions are transferred.

REPORTS TO CONGRESS

SEC. 123. The President from time to time, but not less frequently than once every calendar quarter through 30 June 1952, and once every year thereafter until all operations under this title have been completed, shall transmit to the Congress a report of operations under this title, including the text of bilateral and multilateral agreements entered into in carrying out the provisions of this title. Reports provided for under this section shall be transmitted to the Secretary of the Senate or the Clerk of the House of Representatives, as the case may be, if the Senate or the House of Representatives, as the case may be, is not in session.

JOINT CONGRESSIONAL COMMITTEE

SEC. 124. (*a*) There is hereby established a joint congressional committee to be known as the Joint Committee on Foreign Economic Co-operation (hereinafter referred to as the committee), to be composed of ten members as follows:

(1) Three members who are members of the Committee on Foreign Relations of the Senate, two from the majority and one from the minority party, to be appointed by the chairman of the committee; two members who are members of the Committee on Appropriations of the Senate, one from the majority and one from the minority party, to be appointed by the chairman of the committee; and

(2) Three members who are members of the Committee on Foreign Affairs of the House, two from the majority and one from the minority party, to be appointed by the chairman of the committee; and two members who are members of the Committee on Appropriations of the House, one from the majority and one from the minority party, to be appointed by the chairman of the committee.

A vacancy in the membership of the committee shall be filled in the same manner as the original selection. The committee shall elect a chairman from among its members.

(*b*) It shall be the function of the committee to make a continuous study of the programs of United States economic assistance to foreign countries, and to review the progress achieved in the execution and administration of such programs. Upon request, the committee shall aid the several standing committees of the Congress having legislative jurisdiction over any part of the programs of United States economic assistance to foreign countries; and it shall make a report to the Senate and the House of Representatives, from time to time, concerning the results of its studies, together with such recommendations as it may deem desirable. The Administrator, at the request of the committee, shall consult with the committee from time to time with respect to his activities under this Act.

(*c*) The committee, or any duly authorized sub-committee thereof, is authorized to hold such hearings, to sit and act at such times and places, to require by subpoena or otherwise the attendance of such witnesses and the production of such books, papers, and documents, to administer such oaths, to take such testimony to procure such printing and binding, and to make such expenditures as it deems advisable. The cost of stenographic services to report such hearings shall not be in excess of 25 cents per hundred words. The provisions of Sections 102 to 104, inclusive, of the Revised Statutes shall apply

E

in case of any failure of any witness to comply with any subpoena or to testify when summoned under authority of this subsection.

(d) The committee is authorized to appoint and, without regard to the Classification Act of 1923, as amended, fix the compensation of such experts, consultants, technicians, and organizations thereof, and clerical and stenographic assistants as it deems necessary and advisable.

(e) There are hereby authorized to be appropriated such sums as may be necessary to carry out the provisions of this section, to be disbursed by the Secretary of the Senate on vouchers signed by the chairman.

SEPARABILITY CLAUSE

SEC. 125. If any provision of this Act or the application of such provision to any circumstances or persons shall be held invalid, the validity of the remainder of the Act and the applicability of such provision to other circumstances or persons shall not be affected thereby.

TITLE II

SEC. 201. This title may be cited as the 'International Children's Emergency Fund Assistance Act of 1948'.

SEC. 202. It is the purpose of this title to provide for the special care and feeding of children by authorizing additional moneys for the International Children's Emergency Fund of the United Nations.

SEC. 203. The President is hereby authorized and directed any time after the date of the enactment of this Act and before 1 July 1949, to make contributions (a) from sums appropriated to carry out the purposes of this title and (b) from sums appropriated to carry out the general purposes of the proviso in the first paragraph of the first section of the joint resolution of 31 May 1947 (Public Law 84, Eightieth Congress), as amended, to the International Children's Emergency Fund of the United Nations for the special care and feeding of children.

SEC. 204. No contribution shall be made pursuant to this title or such joint resolution of 31 May 1947, which would cause the sum of (a) the aggregate amount contributed pursuant to this title and (b) the aggregate amount contributed by the United States pursuant to such joint resolution of 31 May 1947, to exceed whichever of the following sums is the lesser:

(1) 72 per centum of the total resources contributed after 31 May 1947, by all governments, including the United States, for programs carried out under the supervision of such Fund: *Provided,* That in computing the amount of resources contributed

58

there shall not be included contributions by any government for the benefit of persons located within the territory of such contributing government; or

(2) $100,000,000.

SEC. 205. Funds appropriated for the purposes of such joint resolution of 31 May 1947, shall remain available through 30 June 1949.

SEC. 206. There is hereby authorized to be appropriated to carry out the purposes of this title for the fiscal year ending 30 June 1949, the sum of $60,000,000.

TITLE III

SEC. 301. This title may be cited as the 'Greek-Turkish Assistance Act of 1948'.

SEC. 302. In addition to the amounts authorized to be appropriated under subsection (b) of Section 4 of the Act of 22 May 1947 (61 Stat. 103), there are hereby authorized to be appropriated not to exceed $275,000,000 to carry out the provisions of such Act, as amended.

SEC. 303. (a) Subsection (a) of Section 4 of such Act of 22 May 1947, is hereby amended by adding at the end thereof the following: 'The Reconstruction Finance Corporation is authorized and directed to make additional advances, not to exceed in the aggregate $50,000,000, to carry out the provisions of this Act, as amended, in such manner and in such amounts as the President shall determine. No interest shall be charged on advances made by the Treasury to the Reconstruction Finance Corporation for this purpose.'

(b) Subsection (b) of Section 4 of the said Act is hereby amended by inserting after the word 'repaid' the following: 'without interest'.

SEC. 304. Subsections (2) and (3) of Section 1 of such Act of 22 May 1947, are hereby amended to permit detailing of persons referred to in such subsections to the United States Missions to Greece and Turkey as well as to the governments of those countries. Section 302 of the Act of 27 January 1948 (Public Law 402, Eightieth Congress), and Section 110 (c) of the Economic Co-operation Act of 1948 (relating to investigations of personnel by the Federal Bureau of Investigation) shall be applicable to any person so detailed pursuant to such subsection (2) of such Act of 1947: *Provided*, That any military or civilian personnel detailed under Section 1 of such Act of 1947 may receive such station allowances or additional allowances as the President may prescribe (and payments of such allowances heretofore made are hereby validated).

TITLE IV

SEC. 401 This title may be cited as the 'China Aid Act of 1948'.

SEC. 402. Recognizing the intimate economic and other relationships between the United States and China, and recognizing that disruption following in the wake of war is not contained by national frontiers, the Congress finds that the existing situation in China endangers the establishment of a lasting peace, the general welfare and national interest of the United States, and the attainment of the objectives of the United Nations. It is the sense of the Congress that the further evolution in China of principles of individual liberty, free institutions, and genuine independence rests largely upon the continuing development of a strong and democratic national government as the basis for the establishment of sound economic conditions and for stable international economic relationships. Mindful of the advantages which the United States has enjoyed through the existence of a large domestic market with no internal trade barriers, and believing that similar advantages can accrue to China, it is declared to be the policy of the people of the United States to encourage the Republic of China and its people to exert sustained common efforts which will speedily achieve the internal peace and economic stability in China which are essential for lasting peace and prosperity in the world. It is further declared to be the policy of the people of the United States to encourage the Republic of China in its efforts to maintain the genuine independence and the administrative integrity of China, and to sustain and strengthen principles of individual liberty and free institutions in China through a program of assistance based on self-help and co-operation: *Provided*, That no assistance to China herein contemplated shall seriously impair the economic stability of the United States. It is further declared to be the policy of the United States that assistance provided by the United States under this title should at all times be dependent upon co-operation by the Republic of China and its people in furthering the program: *Provided further*, That assistance furnished under this title shall not be construed as an express or implied assumption by the United States of any responsibility for policies, acts, or undertakings of the Republic of China or for conditions which may prevail in China at any time.

SEC. 403. Aid provided under this title shall be provided under the applicable provisions of the Economic Co-operation Act of 1948 which are consistent with the purposes of this title. It is not the purpose of this title that China, in order to receive aid hereunder, shall adhere to a joint program for European recovery.

SEC. 404. (*a*) In order to carry out the purposes of this title, there is hereby authorized to be appropriated to the President for aid to

China a sum not to exceed $338,000,000 to remain available for obligation for the period of one year following the date of enactment of this Act.

(b) There is also hereby authorized to be appropriated to the President a sum not to exceed $125,000,000 for additional aid to China through grants, on such terms as the President may determine and without regard to the provisions of the Economic Co-operation Act of 1948, to remain available for obligation for the period of one year following the date of enactment of this Act.

SEC. 405. An agreement shall be entered into between China and the United States containing those undertakings by China which the Secretary of State, after consultation with the Administrator for Economic Co-operation, may deem necessary to carry out the purposes of this title and to improve commercial relations with China.

SEC. 406. Notwithstanding the provisions of any other law, the Reconstruction Finance Corporation is authorized and directed, until such time as an appropriation is made pursuant to Section 404, to make advances, not to exceed in the aggregate $50,000,000, to carry out the provisions of this title in such manner and in such amounts as the President shall determine. From appropriations authorized under Section 404, there shall be repaid without interest to the Reconstruction Finance Corporation the advances made by it under the authority contained herein. No interest shall be charged on advances made by the Treasury to the Reconstruction Finance Corporation in implementation of this section.

SEC. 407. (a) The Secretary of State, after consultation with the Administrator, is hereby authorized to conclude an agreement with China establishing a Joint Commission on Rural Reconstruction in China, to be composed of two citizens of the United States appointed by the President of the United States and three citizens of China appointed by the President of China. Such Commission shall, subject to the direction and control of the Administrator, formulate and carry out a program for reconstruction in rural areas of China, which shall include such research and training activities as may be necessary or appropriate for such reconstruction: Provided, That assistance furnished under this section shall not be construed as an express or implied assumption by the United States of any responsibility for making any further contributions to carry out the purposes of this section.

(b) Insofar as practicable, an amount equal to not more than 10 per centum of the funds made available under subsection (a) of Section 404 shall be used to carry out the purposes of subsection (a) of this section. Such amount may be in United States dollars, proceeds in Chinese currency from the sale of commodities made available to

China with funds authorized under subsection (*a*). of Section 404, or both.

Approved 3 April 1948.

AMENDMENT[1] TO ECONOMIC CO-OPERATION ACT OF 1948

Be it enacted by the Senate and House of Representatives of the United States of America in Congress assembled, That the fourth and fifth sentences of Section 102 (*a*) of the Economic Co-operation Act of 1948 are hereby amended to read as follows: 'Mindful of the advantages which the United States has enjoyed through the existence of a large domestic market with no internal trade barriers, and believing that similar advantages can accrue to the countries of Europe, it is declared to be the policy of the people of the United States to encourage these countries through their joint organization to exert sustained common efforts to achieve speedily that economic co-operation in Europe which is essential for lasting peace and prosperity. It is further declared to be the policy of the people of the United States to encourage the unification of Europe, and to sustain and strengthen principles of individual liberty, free institutions, and genuine independence in Europe through assistance to those countries of Europe which participate in a joint recovery program based upon self-help and mutual co-operation: *Provided,* That no assistance to the participating countries herein contemplated shall seriously impair the economic stability of the United States.'

SEC. 2. The second sentence of Section 104 (*e*) of such Act is hereby amended by striking out '$10,000 per annum' and inserting in lieu thereof 'the highest rate authorized by such Act'.

SEC. 3. The first sentence of Section 105 (*c*) of such Act is hereby amended by striking out 'Section 6 of the Act of 2 July 1940 (54 Stat. 714), as amended,' and inserting in lieu thereof 'the Export Control Act of 1949'.

SEC. 4. Section 108 of such Act is hereby amended by adding at the end thereof the following new sentences: 'There shall be a Deputy United States Special Representative in Europe who shall (*a*) be appointed by the President, by and with the advice and consent of the Senate, (*b*) be entitled to receive the same compensation and allowances as a chief of mission, class 3, within the meaning of the Act of 13 August 1946 (60 Stat. 999), and (*c*) have the rank of ambassador extraordinary and plenipotentiary. The Deputy United States Special Representative shall perform such functions as the United States Special Representative shall designate, and shall be Acting United States Special Representative during the absence or disability of the United States Special Representative or in the event

[1] Public Law 47—81st Congress. Chapter 77—1st Session. S.1209.

of a vacancy in the office of United States Special Representative.'

SEC. 5. The last sentence of Section 109 (a) of such Act is hereby amended by striking out the period and inserting in lieu thereof a semicolon and the following: 'and the chief of the special mission shall be entitled to receive the same compensation and allowances as a chief of mission, class 3, or a chief of mission, class 4, within the meaning of the Act of 13 August 1946 (60 Stat. 999), or compensation and allowances in accordance with Section 110 (a) of this title, as the Administrator shall determine to be necessary or appropriate.'

SEC. 6. (a) The last sentence of paragraph (2) of Section 111 (a) of such Act is hereby amended to read as follows: 'The Administrator shall, in providing for the procurement of commodities under authority of this title, take such steps as may be necessary to assure, as far as is practicable, that at least 50 per centum of the gross tonnage of commodities procured out of funds made available under this title and transported to or from the United States on ocean vessels, computed separately for dry bulk carriers, dry cargo liner and tanker services, is so transported on United States flag vessels to the extent such vessels are available at market rates for United States flag vessels; and, in the administration of this provision, the Administrator shall, insofar as practicable and consistent with the purposes of this title, endeavour to secure a fair and reasonable participation by United States flag vessels in cargoes by geographic area.'

(b) Paragraph (3) of Section 111 (b) of such Act is hereby amended in the following particulars:

(1) By inserting after 'projects' a comma and the following: 'including expansion, modernization, or development of existing enterprises' and a comma;

(2) By inserting after 'media' the following: 'consistent with the national interests of the United States';

(3) By striking out in the first proviso 'in the first year after the date of the enactment of this Act does not exceed $15,000,000' and inserting in lieu thereof 'made in any fiscal year does not exceed $10,000,000';

(4) By amending subparagraph (i) thereof to read as follows:
'(i) the guaranty to any person shall not exceed the amount of dollars invested in the project by such person with the approval of the Administrator plus actual earnings or profits on said project to the extent provided by such guaranty;';

(5) By inserting after subparagraph (iii) thereof the following new subparagraphs:
'(iv) as used in this paragraph, the term "investment" includes the furnishing of capital goods items and related services, for use in connection with projects approved by the Administrator,

pursuant to a contract providing for payment in whole or in part after 30 June 1950; and

'(v) the guaranty to any person shall be limited to assuring the transfer into United States dollars of other currencies, or credits in such currencies received by such person as earnings or profits from the approved investment, as repayment or return thereof, in whole or in part, or as compensation for the sale or disposition of all or any part thereof. When any payment is made to any person pursuant to a guaranty as hereinbefore described, the currency or credits on account of which such payment is made shall become the property of the United States Government, and the United States Government shall be subrogated to any right, title, claim, or cause of action existing in connection therewith'; and

(6) By amending the next to last sentence thereof to read as follows: 'The total amount of the guaranties made under this paragraph (3) shall not exceed $150,000,000: *Provided*, That any funds allocated to a guaranty and remaining after all liability of the United States assumed in connection therewith has been released, discharged, or otherwise terminated, shall be available for allocation to other guaranties, the foregoing limitation notwithstanding.'

(c) Paragraph (2) of Section 111 (c) of such Act is hereby amended in the following particulars:

(1) By inserting after the second sentence thereof the following: 'In addition to the amount of notes above authorized, the Administrator is authorized, for the purpose of carrying out the provisions of paragraph (3) of subsection (b) of this section, to issue notes from time to time for purchase by the Secretary of the Treasury in an amount not exceeding in the aggregate $150,000,000 less any amount allocated prior to 3 April 1949 for such purpose, until all liabilities arising under guaranties made pursuant to this authorization have expired or been discharged.';

(2) By striking out the first two words, 'Such notes' in the third sentence thereof and inserting 'The notes hereinabove authorized'; and

(3) By inserting after 'Washington' in the sixth sentence thereof 'for assistance on credit terms'.

SEC. 7. (a) Section 112 (c) of such Act is hereby amended by striking out '25 per centum' and inserting in lieu thereof '12½ per centum'.

(b) Section 112 (d) of such Act is hereby amended by adding after the words 'any agricultural commodity, or product thereof' the following: 'or class, type, or specification thereof'.

(c) Section 112 (g) of such Act is hereby amended by striking out 'Section 6 of the Act of 2 July 1940 (54 Stat. 714), including any amendment thereto,' and 'Section 6 of the Act of 2 July 1940, as amended,' and inserting in lieu thereof 'the Export Control Act of 1949'.

(d) Section 112 of such Act is hereby further amended by adding at the end thereof the following new subsections:

'(i) (1) Insofar as practicable and to the maximum extent consistent with the accomplishment of the purposes of this title, the Administrator shall assist American small business to participate equitably in the furnishing of commodities and services financed with funds authorized under this title by making available or causing to be made available to suppliers in the United States, and particularly to small independent enterprises, information, as far in advance as possible, with respect to purchases proposed to be financed with funds authorized under this title, and by making available or causing to be made available to prospective purchasers in the participating countries information as to commodities and services produced by small independent enterprises in the United States, and by otherwise helping to give small business an opportunity to participate in the furnishing of commodities and services financed with funds authorized under this title.

'(2) The Administrator shall appoint a special assistant to advise and assist him in carrying out the foregoing paragraph (1). Each report transmitted to the Congress under Section 123 shall include a report of all activities under this subsection.

'(j) The Administrator shall, in providing assistance in the procurement of commodities in the United States, make available United States dollars for marine insurance on such commodities where such insurance is placed on a competitive basis in accordance with normal trade practices prevailing prior to the outbreak of World War II.

'(k) No funds authorized for the purposes of this title shall be used in the United States for advertising foreign products or for advertising foreign travel.

'(1) No funds authorized for the purposes of this title shall be used for the purchase in bulk of any commodities (other than commodities procured by or in the possession of the Commodity Credit Corporation pursuant to price-support programs required by law) at prices higher than the market price prevailing in the United States at the time of the purchase adjusted for differences in the cost of transportation to destination, quality, and terms of payment.'

SEC. 8. (a) Section 114 (c) of such Act is hereby amended in the following particulars:

(1) By striking out the period at the end of the first sentence thereof and inserting in lieu thereof a colon and the following: 'Provided further, That, in addition to the amount heretofore authorized and appropriated, there are hereby authorized to be appropriated for

carrying out the provisions and accomplishing the purposes of this title not to exceed $1,150,000,000 for the period 3 April 1949 through 30 June 1949, and not to exceed $4,280,000,000 for the fiscal year ending 30 June 1950: *Provided further*, That, in addition to the foregoing, any balance, unobligated as of 30 June 1949, or subsequently released from obligation, of funds appropriated for carrying out and accomplishing the purposes of this title for any period ending on or prior to that date is hereby authorized to be made available for obligation through the fiscal year ending 30 June 1950, and to be transferred to and consolidated with any appropriations for carrying out and accomplishing the purposes of this title for said fiscal year.'; and

(2) By amending the last sentence of such Section 114 (*c*) to read as follows: 'The authorizations in this title are limited to the period ending 30 June 1950, in order that the Congress may pass on any subsequent authorizations.'

(*b*) Section 114 of such Act is hereby further amended by adding at the end thereof the following new subsection:

'(*g*) Notwithstanding the provisions of any other law, until such time as an appropriation additional to that made by title I of the Foreign Aid Appropriation Act, 1949 (Public Law 793, Eightieth Congress), shall be made pursuant to subsection (*c*) of this section the Reconstruction Finance Corporation is authorized and directed to make advances not to exceed in the aggregate $1,000,000,000 to carry out the provisions of this title, in such manner, at such times, and in such amounts as the Administrator shall request, and no interest shall be charged on advances made by the Treasury to the Reconstruction Finance Corporation for this purpose. The Reconstruction Finance Corporation shall be repaid without interest for advances made by it hereunder, from funds made available for the purposes of this title.'

SEC. 9. (*a*) Paragraph (6) of Section 115 (*b*) of such Act is hereby amended by striking out the period following the words 'grant basis' and inserting in lieu thereof a colon and the following: '*Provided*, That the obligation to make such deposits may be waived, in the discretion of the Administrator, with respect to technical information or assistance furnished under Section 111 (*a*) (3) of this title and with respect to ocean transportation furnished on United States flag vessels under Section 111 of this title in an amount not exceeding the amount, as determined by the Administrator, by which the charges for such transportation exceed the cost of such transportation at world market rates.'

(*b*) Such Section 115 (*b*) (6) is hereby further amended by inserting after 'or for such other expenditures as may be consistent with' the words 'the declaration of policy contained in Section 102 and'.

(*c*) Section 115 (*d*) of such Act is hereby amended to read as follows:

'(*d*) The Administrator shall encourage each participating country to insure, by an effective follow-up system, that efficient use is made of the commodities, facilities, and services furnished under this title. In order further to insure that each participating country makes efficient use of such commodities, facilities, and services, and of its own resources, the Administrator shall encourage the joint organization of the participating countries referred to in subsection (*b*) of this section to observe and review the operation of such follow-up systems.'

(*d*) Section 115 of such Act is hereby further amended by adding two new subsections as follows:

'(*h*) Not less than 5 per centum of each special local currency account established pursuant to paragraph (6) of subsection (*b*) of this section shall be allocated to the use of the United States Government for expenditure for materials which are required by the United States as a result of deficiencies or potential deficiencies in its own resources or for other local currency requirements of the United States.

'(*i*) (1) The Administrator shall, to the greatest extent practicable, initiate projects for and assist the appropriate agencies of the United States Government in procuring and stimulating increased production in participating countries of materials which are required by the United States as a result of deficiencies or potential deficiencies in its own resources; and in furtherance of those objectives the Administrator shall, in addition to the local currency allocated pursuant to subsection (*h*), use such other means available to him under this title as he may deem appropriate.

'(2) In furtherance of such objectives and within the limits of the appropriations and contract authorizations of the Bureau of Federal Supply to procure strategic and critical materials, the Administrator, with the approval of the Director of such Bureau, shall enter into contracts in the name of the United States for the account of such Bureau for the purchase of strategic and critical materials in any participating country. Such contracts may provide for deliveries over definite periods, but not to exceed twenty years in any contract, and may provide for payments in advance of deliveries.

'(3) Nothing in this subsection shall be deemed to restrict or limit in any manner the authority now held by any agency of the United States Government in procuring or stimulating increased production of the materials referred to in paragraphs (1) and (2) in countries other than participating countries.'

SEC. 10. (*a*) The first sentence of Section 117 (*c*) of such Act is hereby amended by striking out the period and inserting in lieu thereof a colon and the following: '*Provided*, That the Administrator shall fix and pay a uniform rate per pound for the ocean transportation of all relief packages of food or other general classification of commodities shipped to any participating foreign country, regardless of methods of shipment and higher rates charged by particular agencies of transportation, but this proviso shall not apply to shipments made by individuals to individuals through the mails.'

(b) Section 117 (d) of such Act is hereby amended by striking out 'Section 6 of the Act of 2 July 1940 (54 Stat. 714), as amended,' and inserting in lieu thereof 'the Export Control Act of 1949'.

(c) Section 117 of such Act is hereby further amended by adding a new subsection to read as follows:

'(e) Whenever the Administrator shall determine that shipping capacity available to Italy is inadequate for such emigration from Italy as may be desirable to further the purposes of this title, the Administrator shall request the United States Maritime Commission to make available to Italy vessels capable of engaging in such service for the purpose of transporting emigrants from Italy to destinations other than the United States, and shall specify the terms and conditions under which such vessels shall thus be made available, and the United States Maritime Commission thereupon shall, notwithstanding any other provisions of law and without reimbursement by the Administrator, make such vessels available to Italy in accordance with such terms and conditions: *Provided,* That the total number of such vessels made available for such purpose shall not at any one time exceed ten: *Provided further,* That title to each such vessel owned by the United States Government shall remain in the United States: *And provided further,* That the terms and conditions under which such vessels are made available to Italy shall obligate Italy to return the vessels forthwith upon demand of the President, and in any event not later than 30 June 1952.'

SEC. 11. The second sentence of Section 118 of such Act is amended by inserting before the period at the end thereof 'or (3) the provision of such assistance would be inconsistent with the obligations of the United States under the Charter of the United Nations to refrain from giving assistance to any State against which the United Nations is taking preventative or enforcement action'.

SEC. 12. An amount, equal to any balance, unobligated as of 2 April 1949, or subsequently released from obligation, of funds appropriated by Public Law 793, approved 28 June 1948, for the purposes of the China Aid Act of 1948 is hereby made available to the President for obligation through 15 February 1950, for assistance in areas in China which he may deem to be not under Communist domination, to be furnished in such manner and on such terms and conditions as he may determine.

Approved 19 April 1949.

CONVENTION FOR EUROPEAN ECONOMIC CO-OPERATION, TOGETHER WITH THE RESOLUTIONS TRANSMITTED TO THE COUNCIL BY THE COMMITTEE OF EUROPEAN ECONOMIC CO-OPERATION[1]

Paris, 16 April 1948

The Governments of Austria, Belgium, Denmark, France, Greece, Ireland, Iceland, Italy, Luxembourg, Norway, the Netherlands, Portugal, the United Kingdom, Sweden, Switzerland and Turkey, and the Commanders-in-Chief of the French, United Kingdom and United States Zones of Occupation of Germany:

Considering that a strong and prosperous European economy is essential for the attainment of the purpose of the United Nations, the preservation of individual liberty and the increase of general well-being, and that it will contribute to the maintenance of peace;

Recognizing that their economic systems are interrelated and that the prosperity of each of them depends on the prosperity of all;

Believing that only by close and lasting co-operation between the Contracting Parties can the prosperity of Europe be restored and maintained, and the ravages of war made good;

Resolved to implement the principles and to achieve the aims set forth in the General Report of the Committee of European Economic Co-operation, particularly the speedy establishment of sound economic conditions enabling the Contracting Parties as soon as possible to achieve and maintain a satisfactory level of economic activity without extraordinary outside assistance, and to make their full contribution to world economic stability;

Determined to combine their economic strength to these ends, to join together to make the fullest collective use of their individual capacities and potentialities, to increase their production, develop and modernize their industrial and agricultural equipment, expand their commerce, reduce progressively barriers to trade among themselves, promote full employment and restore or maintain the stability of their economies and general confidence in their national currencies;

Taking note of the generous resolve of the American people expressed in the action taken to furnish the assistance without which the aims set forth above cannot be fully achieved;

Resolved to create the conditions and establish the institutions

[1] Cmd. 7388.

necessary for the success of European economic co-operation and for the effective use of American aid, and to conclude a Convention to this end;

Have accordingly appointed the undersigned Plenipotentiaries who, having presented their full powers, found in good and due form, have agreed on the following provisions:

Article 1

The Contracting Parties agree to work in close co-operation in their economic relations with one another.

As their immediate task, they will undertake the elaboration and execution of a joint recovery programme. The object of this programme will be to achieve as soon as possible and maintain a satisfactory level of economic activity without extraordinary outside assistance, and to this end the programme will take special account of the need of the Contracting Parties to develop their exports to non-participating countries to the maximum extent possible.

Accordingly the Contracting Parties pledge themselves to carry out, by their efforts of self-help and in a spirit of mutual aid, the following General Obligations, and hereby set up an Organization for European Economic Co-operation, hereinafter referred to as the Organization.

PART I—GENERAL OBLIGATIONS

Article 2

The Contracting Parties will, both individually and collectively, promote with vigour the development of production, through efficient use of the resources at their command, whether in their metropolitan or overseas territories, and by the progressive modernization of equipment and techniques, in such manner as may best assist the accomplishment of the joint recovery programme.

Article 3

The Contracting Parties will, within the framework of the Organization and as often and to such extent as may be necessary, draw up general programmes for the production and exchange of commodities and services. In so doing they will take into consideration their several estimates or programmes and general world economic conditions.

Each Contracting Party will use its best endeavours to secure the fulfilment of such general programmes.

Article 4

The Contracting Parties will develop, in mutual co-operation, the maximum possible interchange of goods and services. To this end they will continue the efforts already initiated to achieve as soon as possible a multilateral system of payments among themselves, and will co-operate in relaxing restrictions on trade and payments between one another, with the object of abolishing as soon as possible those restrictions which at present hamper such trade and payments.

In the application of this Article, the Contracting Parties will take due account of the necessity that they should, collectively and individually, correct or avoid excessive disequilibrium in their financial and economic relations, both amongst themselves and with non-participating countries.

Article 5

The Contracting Parties agree to strengthen their economic links by all methods which they may determine will further the objectives of the present Convention. They will continue the study of Customs Unions or analogous arrangements such as free trade areas, the formation of which might constitute one of the methods of achieving these objectives. Those Contracting Parties which have already agreed in principle to the creation of Customs Unions will further the establishment of such Unions as rapidly as conditions permit.

Article 6

The Contracting Parties will co-operate with one another and with other like-minded countries in reducing tariff and other barriers to the expansion of trade, with a view to achieving a sound and balanced multilateral trading system such as will accord with the principles of the Havana Charter.[1]

Article 7

Each Contracting Party will, having due regard to the need for a high and stable level of trade and employment and for avoiding or countering the dangers of inflation, take such steps as lie within its power to achieve or maintain the stability of its currency and of its internal financial position, sound rates of exchange and, generally, confidence in its monetary system.

Article 8

The Contracting Parties will make the fullest and most effective use of their available man-power.

They will endeavour to provide full employment for their own people and they may have recourse to man-power available in the territory of any other Contracting Party. In the latter case they will, in mutual agreement, take the necessary measures to facilitate the

[1] Cmd. 7375.

71

movement of workers and to ensure their establishment in conditions satisfactory from the economic and social point of view.

Generally, the Contracting Parties will co-operate in the progressive reduction of obstacles to the free movement of persons.

Article 9

The Contracting Parties will furnish the Organization with all the information it may request of them in order to facilitate the accomplishment of its tasks.

PART II—THE ORGANIZATION

Article 10

Membership

The Members of the Organization shall be the Parties to the present Convention.

Article 11

Aim

The aim of the Organization shall be the achievement of a sound European economy through the economic co-operation of its members. An immediate task of the Organization will be to ensure the success of the European recovery programme, in accordance with the undertakings contained in Part I of the present Convention.

Article 12

Functions

Within the limits of such powers as are or may be agreed for the Organization, its functions shall be:—

(*a*) to prepare and implement, within the sphere of the collective action of the Members concerned, the measures necessary to achieve the aim laid down in Article 11 and to facilitate, promote and co-ordinate the individual action of the Members;

(*b*) to facilitate and review the implementation of the present Convention; to take such action as may be found appropriate in order to ensure its execution; and to this end, to provide for systems of observation and review adequate to ensure the efficient use both of external aid and of indigenous resources;

(*c*) to provide the United States Government with such assistance and information as may be agreed in relation to the execution of the European recovery programme and to address recommendations to that Government;

(*d*) at the request of the interested parties, to assist in the negotiation of such international agreements as may be necessary for the better execution of the European recovery programme.

The Organization may also assume such other functions as may be agreed.

Article 13
Powers

In order to achieve its aim as set out in Article 11 the Organization may:

(a) take decisions for implementation by Members;

(b) enter into agreements with its Members, non-member countries, the United States Government and International Organizations;

(c) make recommendations to the United States Government, to other Governments, and to International Organizations.

Article 14
Decisions

Unless the Organization otherwise agrees for special cases, decisions shall be taken by mutual agreement of all the Members. The abstention of any Members declaring themselves not to be interested in the subject under discussion shall not invalidate decisions, which shall be binding for the other Members.

Article 15
The Council

(a) A Council composed of all the Members shall be the body from which all decisions derive.

(b) The Council shall designate annually from among the Members a Chairman and two Vice-Chairmen.

(c) The Council shall be assisted by an Executive Committee and a Secretary-General. The Council may set up such technical committees or other bodies as may be required for the performance of the functions of the Organization. All such organs shall be responsible to the Council.

Article 16
The Executive Committee

(a) The Executive Committee shall consist of seven Members to be designated annually by the Council. It shall carry on its work in accordance with the general and specific instructions of the Council and shall report on it to the Council.

(b) The Council shall designate annually from among the Members of the Executive Committee a Chairman and a Vice-Chairman. It may also designate annually a Rapporteur-General and specify his functions.

(c) Any member of the Organization not represented on the

F

Executive Committee may take part in all the discussions and decisions of that Committee on any item specially affecting the interests of that Member.

The Members of the Organization shall be informed of the proceedings of the Executive Committee by the circulation in good time of agenda and summary records.

Article 17
The Secretary-General

(a) The Secretary-General shall be assisted by a first and a second Deputy Secretary-General.

(b) The Secretary-General and the Deputy Secretaries-General shall be appointed by the Council. The Secretary-General shall be under the instructions of the Council.

(c) The Secretary-General shall attend or be represented at the meetings of the Council, the Executive Committee and, as required, at meetings of the technical committees and the other bodies, with the right to participate in discussion. He will prepare the meetings of the Council and of the Executive Committee and will ensure the execution of their decisions in accordance with the general and specific instructions of the Council and the Executive Committee.

Additional provisions as to the functions of the Secretary-General are set out in the Annex to the present Convention.

Article 18
Secretariat

(a) The Secretary-General shall appoint such staff as the Organization may require. Senior staff appointments and the staff regulations shall be subject to approval by the Council.

(b) Having regard to the international character of the Organization, the Secretary-General and the staff shall neither seek nor receive instructions from any of the Members or from any Government or authority external to the Organization.

Article 19
Technical Committees and Other Bodies

Technical committees and other bodies set up under Article 15 (c) shall be under the instructions of the Council. They shall be composed of the Members most concerned and will so organize their work that other interested Members may take part as may be necessary.

Article 20
Relationships with Other International Organizations

(a) The Organization shall establish such formal or informal relationships with the United Nations, its principal organs and subsidiary bodies and with the Specialized Agencies as may best facilitate collaboration in the achievement of their respective aims.

(b) The Organization may also maintain relationships with other international bodies.

Article 21

Headquarters

The Headquarters of the Organization shall be determined by the Council at its first session.

The Council, the several committees or the other bodies may meet elsewhere than at the Headquarters of the Organization should they so decide.

Article 22

Legal Capacity, Privileges, and Immunities

(a) The Organization shall enjoy in the territory of each of its Members such legal capacity as may be necessary for the exercise of its functions and the fulfilment of its purposes, as defined in Supplementary Protocol No. I to the present Convention.

(b) The Organization, its officials and representatives of the Members of the Organization shall be entitled to the privileges and immunities set out in the above-mentioned Supplementary Protocol.

Article 23

Financial Regulations

(a) The Secretary-General shall present to the Council for approval an annual budget and accounts drawn up in accordance with the Financial Regulations set out in Supplementary Protocol No. II to the present Convention.

(b) The financial year of the Organization shall begin on 1 July.

(c) The expenses of the Organization shall be borne by Members and shall be apportioned in accordance with the provisions of the above-mentioned Supplementary Protocol.

Part III—Final Clauses

Article 24

Ratification and Coming into Force

(a) The present Convention shall be ratified. Instruments of ratification shall be deposited with the Government of the French Republic. The Convention shall come into force upon the deposit of instruments of ratification by not less than six of the signatories. For each signatory ratifying thereafter, the Convention shall come into force upon the deposit of its instrument of ratification.

(b) Nevertheless, pending the coming into force of the Convention in the manner provided by the preceding paragraph, the signatories agree, in order to avoid delay in its execution, to put it into operation on signature on a provisional basis and in accordance with their several constitutional requirements.

Article 25
Accession

At any time after not less than ten instruments of ratification of the present Convention have been deposited, any non-signatory European country may accede to it by notification addressed to the Government of the French Republic, and with the assent of the Council of the Organization. Accessions shall take effect on the date of such assent.

Article 26
Non-Fulfilment of Obligations

If any Member of the Organization ceases to fulfil its obligations under the present Convention, it shall be invited to conform to the provisions of the Convention. If the said Member should not so conform within the period indicated in the invitation, the other Members may decide, by mutual agreement, to continue their co-operation within the Organization without that Member.

Article 27
Withdrawal

Any of the Contracting Parties may terminate the application of the present Convention to itself by giving twelve months' notice to that effect to the Government of the French Republic.

Article 28
Communication of Ratifications, Accessions, and Withdrawals

Upon the receipt of any instrument of ratification or accession, or of any notice of withdrawal, the Government of the French Republic shall give notice thereof to all the Contracting Parties and to the Secretary-General of the Organization.

ANNEX

ADDITIONAL PROVISIONS CONCERNING THE FUNCTIONS OF THE SECRETARY-GENERAL

Provisions concerning the functions of the Secretary-General additional to those specified in Article 17 are set out below:—

(1) He may submit proposals to the Council and to the Executive Committee.

(2) He shall provide, in agreement with the Chairmen of the technical committees, for these committees to be convened as required and for the necessary secretarial arrangements. He shall transmit to them, as necessary, the instructions of the Council and of the Executive Committee.

(3) He shall follow the work of the other bodies referred to in Article 15 (c) and transmit to them, as necessary, the instructions of the Council and of the Executive Committee.

(4) He shall, having regard to the provisions of Article 20 and in accordance with the instructions of the Council and the Executive Committee, make the necessary arrangements for liaison with other International Organizations.

(5) He shall exercise all such other functions necessary for the efficient administration of the Organization as may be entrusted to him by the Council or by the Executive Committee.

In faith whereof the undersigned Plenipotentiaries, being duly authorized to that effect, have signed the present Convention and have affixed thereto their Seals.

Done in Paris this sixteenth day of April, Nineteen Hundred and Forty-Eight, in the English and French languages, both texts being equally authentic, in a single copy which shall remain deposited in the Archives of the Government of the French Republic, by which certified copies will be communicated to all the other signatories.

[Here follow the Signatures]

SUPPLEMENTARY PROTOCOL NO. I TO THE CONVENTION FOR EUROPEAN ECONOMIC CO-OPERATION ON THE LEGAL CAPACITY, PRIVILEGES, AND IMMUNITIES OF THE ORGANIZATION

The Government and Authorities signatories to the Convention for European Economic Co-operation:

Considering that, according to the provisions of Article 22 of the Convention, the Organization for European Economic Co-operation shall enjoy in the territory of each of its Members such legal capacity as may be necessary for the exercise of its functions and the fulfilment of its purposes, and that the Organization, its officials, and representatives of the Members of the Organization shall be entitled to the privileges and immunities set out in a Supplementary Protocol;

Have agreed on the following provisions:—

Part I—Personality, Capacity

Article 1

The Organization shall possess juridical personality. It shall have the capacity to conclude contracts, to acquire and dispose of movable and immovable property and to institute legal proceedings.

Part II—Property, Funds, and Assets

Article 2

The Organization, its property, and assets wherever located and by whomsoever held, shall enjoy immunity from every form of legal process except in so far as in any particular case it has expressly waived its immunity. It is, however, understood that no waiver of immunity shall extend to any measure of execution.

Article 3

The premises of the Organization shall be inviolable. The property and assets of the Organization, wherever located and by whomsoever held, shall be immune from search, requisition, confiscation, expropriation and any other form of interference, whether by executive, administrative, judicial, or legislative action.

Article 4

The archives of the Organization, and in general all documents belonging to it or held by it, shall be inviolable wherever located.

Article 5

Without being restricted by financial controls, regulations, or moratoria of any kind:

(*a*) the Organization may hold currency of any kind and operate accounts in any currency;

(*b*) the Organization may freely transfer its funds from one country to another or within any country and convert any currency held by it into any other currency.

Article 6

The Organization, its assets, income, and other property shall be:

(*a*) exempt from all direct taxes; it is understood, however, that the Organization will not claim exemption from rates and taxes which are in fact no more than charges for public utility services;

(*b*) exempt from customs duties and prohibitions and restrictions on imports and exports in respect of articles imported or exported by the Organization for its official use. It is understood, however, that articles imported under such exemption will not be sold in the country into which they were imported except under conditions agreed with the Government of that country;

(c) exempt from customs duties and prohibitions and restrictions on imports and exports in respect of its publications.

Article 7

While the Organization will not, as a general rule, claim exemption from excise duties and from taxes on the sale of movable and immovable property which form part of the price to be paid, nevertheless when the Organization is making important purchases for official use of property on which such duties and taxes have been charged or are chargeable, Members will, whenever possible, make appropriate administrative arrangements for the remission or return of the amount of duty or tax.

PART III—FACILITIES IN RESPECT OF COMMUNICATIONS

Article 8

The Organization shall enjoy in the territory of each Member, for its official communications, treatment not less favourable than that accorded by the Government of that Member to any other Government including its diplomatic mission in the matter of priorities, rates and taxes on mails, cables, telegrams, radiograms, telephotos, telephone and other communications and press rates for information to the press and radio. No censorship shall be applied to the official correspondence and other official communications of the Organization.

PART IV—THE REPRESENTATIVES OF MEMBERS

Article 9

Representatives of Members to the principal and subsidiary organs of the Organization shall, while exercising their functions and during their journey to and from the place of meeting, enjoy the privileges, immunities and facilities normally enjoyed by the diplomatic envoys of comparable rank.

Article 10

Privileges, immunities, and facilities are accorded to the representatives of Members not for the personal benefit of the individuals concerned, but in order to safeguard the independent exercise of their functions in connection with the Organization. Consequently, a Member has not only the right but the duty to waive the immunity of its representative in any case where, in the opinion of the Member, the immunity would impede the course of justice, and it can be waived without prejudice to the purpose for which the immunity is accorded.

Article 11

The provisions of Article 9 are not applicable as between a representative and the authorities of the State of which he is a national or of which he is or has been the representative.

Article 12

In this Part IV the expression 'representatives' shall be deemed to include all delegates, alternates, advisers, technical experts, and secretaries of delegations.

PART V—OFFICIALS

Article 13

The Secretary-General will specify the categories of officials to which the provisions of this Part V shall apply. He shall submit a list of these categories to the Council. Thereafter this list shall be communicated to all Members. The names of the officials included in these categories shall from time to time be made known to Members.

Article 14

Officials of the Organization shall:

(a) be immune from legal process in respect of things done by them in their official capacity; they shall continue to be so immune after completion of their functions as officials of the Organization;

(b) enjoy the same exemption from taxation in respect of the salaries and emoluments paid to them as is enjoyed by officials of the principal International Organizations and on the same conditions;

(c) be immune, together with their spouses and dependent relatives, from immigration restrictions and alien registration;

(d) be accorded the same privileges in respect of exchange facilities as are accorded to the officials of comparable rank forming a part of diplomatic missions;

(e) be given, together with their spouses and dependent relatives, the same repatriation facilities in time of international crisis as members of diplomatic missions;

(f) have the right to import free of duty their furniture and effects at the time of first taking up their post in the country in question.

Article 15

In addition to the privileges, immunities, exemptions, and facilities specified in Article 14, the Secretary-General shall be accorded in respect of himself, his spouse, and children under the age of twenty-one, the privileges, immunities, exemptions, and facilities accorded to heads of diplomatic missions in conformity with international law. The Deputy Secretaries-General shall enjoy the privileges, immunities, exemptions, and facilities accorded to diplomatic representatives of comparable rank.

Article 16

Privileges, immunities, and facilities are granted to officials in the interests of the Organization and not for the personal benefit of the individuals concerned. The Secretary-General shall have the right and the duty to waive the immunity of any official in any case where, in his opinion, the immunity would impede the course of justice and can be waived without prejudice to the interests of the Organization. In the case of the Secretary-General and the Deputy Secretaries-General the Council shall have the right to waive immunity.

Article 17

The Organization shall co-operate at all times with the appropriate authorities of Members to facilitate the proper administration of justice, secure the observance of police regulations and prevent the occurrence of any abuse in connection with the privileges, immunities, exemptions, and facilities mentioned in this Part V.

Part VI—Experts on Missions for the Organization

Article 18

Experts (other than officials coming within the scope of Part V) performing missions for the Organization shall be accorded such privileges, immunities, and facilities as are necessary for the independent exercise of their functions during the period of their missions, including the time spent on journeys in connection with their missions. In particular they shall be accorded—

(a) immunity from personal arrest or detention and from seizure of their baggage;

(b) in respect of things done by them in the course of the performance of their mission, immunity from legal process of every kind;

(c) inviolability for all papers and documents.

Article 19

Privileges, immunities, and facilities are granted to experts in the interests of the Organization and not for the personal benefit of the individuals concerned. The Secretary-General shall have the right and the duty to waive the immunity of any expert in any case where, in his opinion, the immunity would impede the course of justice and it can be waived without prejudice to the interests of the Organization.

PART VII—SUPPLEMENTARY AGREEMENTS

Article 20

The Organization may conclude with any Member or Members supplementary agreements adjusting the provisions of the present Protocol so far as that Member or those Members are concerned.

In faith whereof the undersigned Plenipotentiaries, being duly authorized to that effect, have signed the present Protocol.

Done in Paris this sixteenth day of April, Nineteen Hundred and Forty-Eight, in the English and French languages, both texts being equally authentic, in a single copy which shall remain deposited in the Archives of the Government of the French Republic, by which certified copies will be communicated to all the other signatories.

[*Here follow the Signatures*]

SUPPLEMENTARY PROTOCOL No. II TO THE CONVENTION FOR EUROPEAN ECONOMIC CO-OPERATION ON THE FINANCIAL REGULATIONS OF THE ORGANIZATION

The Governments and Authorities signatories to the Convention for European Economic Co-operation:

Considering that Article 23 of the Convention provides that a Supplementary Protocol on Financial Regulations of the Organization for European Economic Co-operation shall be drawn up;

Have agreed on the following provisions:—

Article 1

Budget

The Secretary-General shall not later than 1 May in each year submit to the Council for consideration and approval detailed estimates of expenditure for the following financial year.

Estimates of expenditure shall be divided under general headings. Transfers within the budget shall not be permitted except by authority of the Executive Committee. The exact form of estimates shall be determined by the Secretary-General.

Travelling and subsistence expenses of representatives of Members shall normally be borne by the Members concerned. The Council may authorize the reimbursement in special cases of expenditure incurred by representatives of Members in connection with special tasks laid upon them by the Organization.

Article 2
Supplementary Budget

The Council may require the Secretary-General to present a supplementary budget if circumstances make it necessary. The Secretary-General shall submit to the Council an estimate of the cost of all resolutions submitted to the Council. No resolution involving additional expenditure shall be deemed to be approved by the Council until it has approved an estimate of the additional expenditure involved.

Article 3
Budget Committee

A Budget Committee composed of representatives of Members of the Organization shall be set up by the Council. The Secretary-General shall submit the budget to this Committee for preliminary examination before submitting it to the Council.

Article 4
Basis of Contributions

Approved budget expenditure shall be met by contributions from the Members of the Organization in accordance with a scale approved by the Council.

The Secretary-General shall notify the amount of their contributions to Members and invite them to remit their contribution at a date to be fixed by him.

Article 5
Currency of Contributions

The budget of the Organization shall be expressed in the currency of the country in which the Headquarters of the Organization are established. The contributions of Members shall be made in that currency.

The Council may, however, require Members to pay a fraction of their contributions in any currency which may be needed for the work of the Organization.

Article 6
Working Capital Fund

Until the contributions have been assessed and paid, the Council shall call upon Members from time to time as may be necessary to make advances of working capital in the same currency or currencies as the contributions. These advances shall be reimbursed during the same financial year by appropriate deductions from contributions. The amount of such advances shall be assessed on the basis of the criterion used in calculating the contributions themselves.

Article 7
Accounts and Auditing

The Secretary-General shall cause an accurate account to be kept of all receipts and disbursements.

The Council shall appoint auditors who will serve for three years in the first instance and may be reappointed. The function of the auditors shall be to examine the accounts of the Organization particularly in order to certify that expenditure has conformed to the provisions made in the budget.

The Secretary-General shall furnish the auditors with such facilities as they may require to carry out their duties.

Article 8
Financial Regulations

The Secretary-General shall submit to the Council for approval as soon as possible after the establishment of the Organization detailed financial regulations drawn up in accordance with the principles set out herein and designed to ensure sound financial administration and economy of expenditure.

Article 9
Provisional Budget

Exceptionally, the Secretary-General shall, not later than two months after the coming into force of the Convention, present to the Council a first budget which will cover the period from the coming into force of the Convention up to 30 June 1949, together with proposals regarding the amount of the advances of working capital required.

In faith whereof the undersigned Plenipotentiaries, being duly authorized to that effect, have signed the present Protocol.

Done in Paris this sixteenth day of April, Nineteen Hundred and Forty-Eight, in the English and French languages, both texts being equally authentic, in a single copy which shall remain deposited in the Archives of the Government of the French Republic, by which certified copies will be communicated to all the other signatories.

[Here follow the Signatures]

RESOLUTIONS TRANSMITTED TO THE COUNCIL BY THE COMMITTEE OF EUROPEAN ECONOMIC CO-OPERATION

RESOLUTION 1: ON THE FUNCTIONS OF THE ORGANIZATION FOR EUROPEAN ECONOMIC CO-OPERATION

The Committee of European Economic Co-operation:

Considering that the Organization which is to be set up by the

Convention for European Economic Co-operation will be entrusted with the functions specified in Article 12 of that Convention;

And considering it desirable to define the tasks of the Organization, within the framework of these functions;

Recommends that the Organization should in particular assume the following tasks to the fullest extent possible:—

(1) to prepare as often as necessary, on the basis of and after examination of national estimates or programmes, such general production, import and export programmes as appear necessary to further the objects of the Convention;

(2) to consider, in the light of national estimates or programmes of development submitted by the Contracting Parties, the best use of productive capacity and man-power to further the objects of the Convention within both their metropolitan and overseas territories, and the measures necessary to achieve these ends;

(3) to promote consultation between the countries concerned, to consider the measures and create the machinery necessary for European economic co-operation especially in matters of trade, international payments, and movement of labour;

(4) to investigate, wherever necessary, methods of co-ordinating the purchasing policies of Members;

(5) to assist Members, at their request, to surmount difficulties incurred in the execution of the European recovery programme;

(6) to make recommendations, as may be appropriate, to the United States Government and, as need be, to other Governments or International Organizations, on the allocation of commodities among the Members, having due regard to the allocating functions of other International Organizations;

(7) to ensure the most efficient use of external aid and to contribute towards ensuring the most efficient use of indigenous resources;

(8) to prepare as often as necessary reports on the execution of the European recovery programme and the use of external aid;

(9) to collect all such information as may facilitate the accomplishment of the tasks of the Organization, having regard to Article 9 of the Convention.

RESOLUTION 2: ON THE RELATIONS BETWEEN THE ORGANIZATION AND THE UNITED STATES SPECIAL REPRESENTATIVE IN EUROPE

The Committee of European Economic Co-operation:

Recommends that the Organization for European Economic Co-operation should make all such arrangements as may be appropriate to maintain close relationships with the United States Special Representative in Europe appointed in accordance with the United

States Economic Co-operation Act of 1948, and to assist him in the performance of his duties.

RESOLUTION 3: ON THE RULES OF PROCEDURE OF THE ORGANIZATION

The Committee of European Economic Co-operation:

Considering that it is for the Council to determine the rules of procedure of the Organization;

Transmits to the Council the following rules of procedure for its consideration:—

Article 1
Meetings

(a) The conduct of meetings shall be in the hands of the Chairman.

(b) At all meetings the presence of a majority of members of the Council or of the Executive Committee or of the technical committees or the other bodies concerned shall suffice for opening the proceedings.

(c) The Council and Executive Committee shall meet as necessary to complete their business satisfactorily; they shall in any case meet at the call of the Chairman or at the request of any one of their members.

Article 2
Agenda

Any Member of the Organization shall have the right to place an item on the agenda. In the case of a Member not represented on a given committee, the chairman concerned shall be consulted before an item is placed on the agenda. Agenda shall be circulated to all Members in good time.

Article 3
Records

The Secretariat shall circulate in good time summary records of the proceedings of the Council, Executive Committee, technical committees and other bodies of the Organization, together with the texts of any decisions, recommendations, or resolutions.

Article 4
Languages

English and French shall be the official and working languages of the Organization.

Article 5
Publicity

The meetings of the Council shall not normally be held in public. The Council may, however, decide that a particular meeting or meetings shall be held in public. The meetings of Committees and other bodies shall not normally be held in public.

Article 6
Amendments

These Rules may be amended by the Council.

RESOLUTION 4: ON THE FINANCING OF THE INITIAL BUDGET OF THE ORGANIZATION

The Committee of European Economic Co-operation:

Considering that Article 23 of the Convention for European Economic Co-operation provides that the expenses of the Organization shall be borne by Members, and that Article 4 of Supplementary Protocol No. II on Financial Regulations stipulates that contributions shall be in accordance with a scale approved by the Council;

Considering that the preparation of this scale will take considerable time and careful consideration; and

Considering that the provision of funds for the initial budget of the Organization requires that Members shall be asked, as soon as the Convention comes into force, for advances to the Working Capital Fund for the first financial year;

Recommends that the Council call up contributions to the Working Capital Fund for the first financial year on the basis of the annexed provisional scale, it being understood that the final scale, which will be subsequently adopted by the Council, shall have retroactive effect and shall completely supersede the provisional scale.

RESOLUTION 5: ON THE INTERIM FINANCING OF THE ORGANIZATION

The Committee of European Economic Co-operation:

Considering that, in accordance with Article 24 (b) of the Convention for European Economic Co-operation, the Council and Committees set up by the said Convention should be in a position to begin operations immediately it is signed and before it comes into force;

Requests the Government of the country where the Organization has its Headquarters to provide, in conformity with the constitutional procedure of that country, the funds necessary to cover the expenses involved in the application of the Convention on a provisional basis; it being understood that the amount so expended shall be deducted from that Government's future contributions to the Organization;

Requests the above-mentioned Government to nominate an official to administer the funds allocated for the provisional application of the Convention;

Decides that a Committee consisting of representatives of three Members of the Organization, to be designated by the Council, be set up to examine estimated expenditure for the period under consideration.

PROVISIONAL SCALE OF CONTRIBUTIONS BY MEMBERS OF THE ORGANIZATION

Member	1 Actual percentage contributions of Members to the United Nations Per cent	2 Nominal percentage contributions of non-Members of the United Nations Per cent	3 Recapitulation Per cent	4 Provisional percentage contributions of Members of the Organization Per cent
Austria	—	0·66	0·66	1·75
Belgium	1·35	—	1·35	3·60
Combined United States/ United Kingdom Zone	—	4·90	4·90	13·20
Denmark..	0·79	—	0·79	2·10
France	6·00	—	6·00	16·20
Greece	0·17	—	0·17	0·45
Ireland	—	0·33	0·33	0·87
Iceland	0·04	—	0·04	0·10
Italy	—	2·95	2·95	8·00
Luxembourg	0·05	—	0·05	0·13
Norway	0·50	—	0·50	1·35
Netherlands	1·40	—	1·40	3·75
Portugal	—	0·99	0·99	2·65
United Kingdom ..	11·48	—	11·48	31·00
Sweden	2·04	—	2·04	5·40
Switzerland	—	1·98	1·98	5·30
Turkey	0·91	—	0·91	2·40
French Zone	—	0·66	0·66	1·75
Total	24·73	12·47	37·20	100·00

NOTE.—The figures in column 1 are drawn from the scale of contributions for 1948 in the budget of the United Nations.

The figures in column 2 are based on a comparison, which is necessarily summary and approximate in character, between those countries which are Members of the United Nations and those countries or territories which are not.

RESOLUTION 6: ON THE STAFF REGULATIONS OF THE ORGANIZATION

The Committee of European Economic Co-operation:

Considering that, according to Article 18 of the Convention for European Economic Co-operation, staff regulations shall be subject to approval by the Council of the Organization;

Transmits to the Council the following draft staff regulations for its consideration:—

PART I—DUTIES AND PRIVILEGES

Article 1

The Secretariat-General of the Organization shall consist of officials whose status shall be international and of subordinate employees. The staff of the Organization shall be under the authority of the Secretary-General and shall be responsible to him in the exercise of their functions.

The Secretary-General shall decide which of the present Regulations shall apply to personnel engaged on a temporary basis to carry out a particular task.

Article 2

Members of the staff of the Organization shall, on appointment, agree to carry out their duties and to regulate their conduct in a manner consistent with the interests of the Organization. They shall obtain the consent of the Secretary-General before accepting any honorary distinction, favour, or monetary award from any Government or from any authority other than the Organization.

The status of the members of the staff of the Organization shall be considered incompatible with employment in any public office of a political character. The discharge by them of any other duty shall be subject to the approval of the Secretary-General.

Members of the staff of the Organization shall abstain from any act, and in particular from making any statement, engaging in public or political activity, or from publishing any matter, which is incompatible with their professional duties and obligations or which would compromise the moral or material responsibility of the Organization.

Article 3

The staff of the Organization shall observe absolute discretion with regard to all official business. They shall not, except in the course of their duties, communicate any information which has not been made public and which has come to their knowledge in the course of their duties, unless they are formally authorized by the Secretary-General to do so.

Article 4

The officials of the Organization shall enjoy the immunities and privileges defined by Supplementary Protocol No. I or by any other agreement negotiated for this purpose. In all cases in which those privileges and immunities are involved, the official concerned shall immediately report to the Secretary-General. When necessary, the Secretary-General shall decide whether or not they shall be waived.

PART II—APPOINTMENTS AND PROMOTIONS

Article 5

Appointment to all posts in the Organization shall be the responsibility of the Secretary-General. Senior Staff appointments shall be subject to approval by the Council.

Article 6

In recruiting staff, the Secretary-General shall primarily bear in mind the necessity for obtaining the services of persons possessing the highest qualities of competence and integrity. He shall provide for as wide a distribution of posts as possible among the nationals of Members of the Organization.

The Secretary-General shall have power to recruit the necessary subordinate personnel at the Headquarters of the Organization.

The appointment of members of the staff of the Organization shall be conditional upon their obtaining from a medical officer, nominated by the Organization, a certificate to the effect that they are not suffering from any infirmity or illness which would prevent them from fulfilling the functions of their appointment.

Article 7

The staff of the Organization shall be engaged by contract. The contract, drawn up in standard form, shall regulate the special terms of employment applicable to each member of the staff.

Article 8

Promotion of members of the staff of the Organization shall be decided by the Secretary-General with due regard to the provisions of Article 5 above.

PART III—SALARIES, ALLOWANCES, LEAVE

Article 9

The Secretary-General shall draw up a list of posts and salary scales, which shall be submitted for the approval of the Council. The list may be revised in the same manner without those concerned being entitled to invoke rights previously accorded them.

Article 10

The Secretary-General shall have power to grant additional allowances to members of the staff who are assigned special responsibilities not corresponding to the normal duties of their grade.

Article 11

Members of the staff of the Organization shall be entitled to family allowances.

Article 12

Travelling expenses and subsistence allowances of members of the staff travelling in the service of the Organization shall be charged to the funds of the Organization.

Article 13

Travelling and removal expenses of members of the staff of the Organization and, in appropriate cases, of their wives and dependent children, shall be paid by the Organization:—

(a) on first appointment to the Secretariat-General and at the time of any further official change of residence;

(b) on termination of their contract.

Nevertheless, in cases of serious offence, the Secretary-General shall be entitled, as a disciplinary measure, to withhold payment or refund, either in whole or in part, of the charges and expenses arising on termination of their contract.

Article 14

Members of the staff shall be entitled to sick leave and maternity leave, and also to annual leave which may from time to time be taken in their country of origin.

Article 15

Any member of the staff of the Organization injured in the exercise of his duties, or obliged to cease work as a result of illness contracted in the exercise thereof, shall receive compensation proportionate to the loss incurred. If any such injury or illness entails death, a gratuity shall be paid to the widow or dependants.

PART IV—TERMINATION OF FUNCTIONS. DISCIPLINE

Article 16

Contracts shall be drawn up for a fixed or indefinite term.

Fixed term contracts shall be subject to six months' probation, during which they can be terminated by either party at one months' notice.

After the expiry of the six months' period the termination of the functions of the contracting member shall take place only on his resignation or as a result of the abolition of a post or posts, subject, nevertheless, to the provisions of Article 18 below.

Such resignation shall enter into force after its acceptance by the Secretary-General.

If the contract is annulled by the abolition of the post, the member of the staff concerned shall receive either three months' notice or payment equivalent to three months' salary.

Article 17

Contracts concluded for an indefinite term may be terminated at any time by either party, subject to notice as specified by the contract and to the provisions of Article 18 below.

Article 18

The Secretary-General may take disciplinary measures against any member of the staff of the Organization guilty of serious misconduct in the course of his duties or otherwise.

Disciplinary measures may consist of reprimand, suspension with or without salary, and dismissal.

PART V—MISCELLANEOUS PROVISIONS

Article 19

Individual disputes arising out of the application of the present Regulations or the execution of contracts of engagement shall be submitted to a committee presided over by a representative of the Council, the other members of which shall be a representative of the Secretary-General and a representative of the staff of the Organization.

Article 20

The execution of the present Regulations shall be defined in rules issued by the Secretary-General, particularly as to working conditions, family allowances, indemnities, refund of expenses, and leave.

Those rules which involve financial expenditure shall be submitted for the approval of the Council.

RESOLUTION 7: ON THE LOCATION OF THE FIRST MEETING OF THE COUNCIL OF THE ORGANIZATION

The Committee of European Economic Co-operation:

Considering that the Convention for European Economic Co-operation does not specify the Headquarters of the Organization;

Resolves that the first meeting of the Council of the Organization shall be held in Paris on 16 April 1948.

SPEECH BY THE RT HON. LOUIS ST LAURENT

(extract)

29 April 1948[1]

What of . . . Canada's relations to the developments towards
western European economic unity and western union? The development and rehabilitation of a sound system of international trade, a
matter of first importance for Canada, is inseparably linked with
European recovery. It must not be forgotten that the United Kingdom and the western European countries have in the past provided
valuable markets for Canadian exports. Should the economies of
these countries collapse, our own economy would suffer a severe
blow. In addition, such a collapse would provide a favourable
environment for Communism which feeds on insecurity, unrest, and
political instability. For these reasons we welcome any development
towards European economic unity, which will in the long run be of
great advantage to Canada by increasing political security and by
widening the area of freer trade.

In so far as widening the area of political security is concerned,
the Prime Minister (Mr Mackenzie King) has already outlined in
this house on 17 March the Government's attitude to the Brussels
five-Power treaty. I think I might repeat here what he then said, to
place it in the context of the world picture. Speaking of the Brussels
five-Power treaty the Prime Minister said:

> This pact is far more than an alliance of the old kind. It is a
> partial realization of the idea of collective security by an arrange-
> ment made under the Charter of the United Nations. As such it
> is a step towards peace, which may well be followed by other
> similar steps until there is built up an association of all free States
> which are willing to accept responsibilities of mutual assistance
> to prevent aggression and preserve peace. . . .
> The Canadian Government has been closely following recent
> developments in the international sphere. The peoples of all free
> countries may be assured that Canada will play her full part in
> every movement to give substance to the conception of an effective
> system of collective security by the development of regional pacts
> under the Charter of the United Nations.

The time has not yet come when it would be wise or useful for

[1] *Debates of the House of Commons, Dominion of Canada*, Session 1948, Vol. 4, p. 3448

the Government to go much beyond that considered and, I think, important statement of Government policy.

I referred to one possible line of development when I spoke seven months ago at the General Assembly. I stated then that it was not necessary to contemplate the break-up of the United Nations or the secession from it of the Soviet group in order to build up a stronger security system within the organization. Without sacrificing the universality of the United Nations, it is possible for the free nations of the world to form their own closer association for collective self-defence under Article 51 of the Charter of the United Nations. Such an association could be created within the United Nations by those free States which are willing to accept more specific and onerous obligations than those contained in the Charter in return for greater national security than the United Nations can now give its members.

It may be that the free States, or some of them, will soon find it necessary to consult together on how best to establish such a collective security league. It might grow out of the plans for 'western union' now maturing in Europe. Its purpose, like that of 'western union', would not be merely negative; it would create a dynamic counter-attraction to Communism—the dynamic counter-attraction of a free, prosperous, and progressive society as opposed to the totalitarian and reactionary society of the Communist world. The formation of such a defensive group of free states would not be a counsel of despair but a measure of hope. It would not mean that we regarded a third world war as inevitable; but that the free democracies had decided that to prevent such a war they would organize so as to confront the forces of Communist expansionism with an overwhelming preponderance of moral, economic, and military force and with sufficient degree of unity to ensure that this preponderance of force is so used that the free nations cannot be defeated one by one. No measure less than this will do. We must at all costs avoid the fatal repetition of the history of the pre-war years when the Nazi aggressor picked off its victims one by one. Such a process does not end at the Atlantic.

I am sure that it is the desire of the people of Canada that Canada should play its full part in creating and maintaining this overwhelming preponderance of moral, economic, and military force and the necessary unity for its effective use.

One thing we must constantly keep in mind as we approach this fateful decision is that the western European democracies are not beggars asking for our charity. They are allies whose assistance we need in order to be able successfully to defend ourselves and our beliefs. Canada and the United States need the assistance of the western European democracies just as they need ours. The spread of aggressive Communist despotism over western Europe would ultimately almost certainly mean for us war, and war on most unfavourable terms. It is in our national interest to see to it that the flood of Communist expansion is held back.

Our foreign policy today must, therefore, I suggest, be based on a recognition of the fact that totalitarian Communist aggression endangers the freedom and peace of every democratic country, including Canada. On this basis and pending the strengthening of the United Nations, we should be willing to associate ourselves with other free states in any appropriate collective security arrangements which may be worked out under Articles 51 or 52 of the Charter.

In the circumstances of the present the organization of collective defence in this way is the most effective guarantee of peace. The pursuit of this course, steadfastly, unprovocatively, and constructively is our best hope for disproving the gloomy predictions of inevitable war.

The burden of maintaining peace, however, will not be easy. We must constantly remember that the union of the free world which is now 'painfully struggling to be born' will possess overwhelming strength only if it is based on moral as well as material force; if its citizens are bound together not merely by a hatred of Communism but by their love of free democracy and their determination to make it work for the promotion of welfare and the preservation of peace.

ECONOMIC CO-OPERATION AGREEMENT[1] BETWEEN THE GOVERNMENTS OF THE UNITED KINGDOM OF GREAT BRITAIN[2] AND NORTHERN IRELAND AND THE UNITED STATES OF AMERICA, WITH ANNEX AND NOTE

London, 6 July 1948

PREAMBLE

The Governments of the United Kingdom of Great Britain and Northern Ireland and of the United States of America:

Recognizing that the restoration or maintenance in European countries of principles of individual liberty, free institutions, and genuine independence rests largely upon the establishment of sound economic conditions, stable international economic relationships, and the achievement by the countries of Europe of a healthy economy independent of extraordinary outside assistance;

Recognizing that a strong and prosperous European economy is essential for the attainment of the purposes of the United Nations;

Considering that the achievement of such conditions calls for a European recovery plan of self-help and mutual co-operation, open to all nations which co-operate in such a plan, based upon a strong production effort, the expansion of foreign trade, the creation or maintenance of internal financial stability and the development of economic co-operation, including all possible steps to establish and maintain valid rates of exchange and to reduce trade barriers;

Considering that in furtherance of these principles the Government of the United Kingdom has joined with other like-minded nations in a Convention for European Economic Co-operation signed at Paris on 16 April 1948,[3] under which the signatories of that Convention agreed to undertake as their immediate task the elaboration and execution of a joint recovery programme, and that the Government of the United Kingdom is a member of the Organization for European Economic Co-operation created pursuant to the provisions of that Convention;

Considering also that, in furtherance of these principles, the Government of the United States of America has enacted the Economic Co-operation Act of 1948, providing for the furnishing of assistance by the United States of America to nations participating

[1] Cmd. 7469.
[2] Similar Agreements were negotiated between the Government of the United States of America and those of nineteen other European countries.
[3] 'Miscellaneous No. 4 (1948),' Cmd. 7388.

in a joint programme for European recovery, in order to enable such nations through their own individual and concerted efforts to become independent of extraordinary outside economic assistance;

Taking note that the Government of the United Kingdom has already expressed its adherence to the purposes and policies of the Economic Co-operation Act of 1948;

Desiring to set forth the understandings which govern the furnishing of assistance by the Government of the United States of America under the Economic Co-operation Act of 1948, the receipt of such assistance by the United Kingdom, and the measures which the two Governments will take individually and together in furthering the recovery of the United Kingdom as an integral part of the joint programme for European recovery.

Have agreed as follows:—

Article I

(1) The Government of the United States of America undertakes to assist the United Kingdom, by making available to the Government of the United Kingdom or to any person, agency, or organization designated by the latter Government such assistance as may be requested by it and approved by the Government of the United States of America. The Government of the United States of America will furnish this assistance under the provisions, and subject to all of the terms, conditions and termination provisions, of the Economic Co-operation Act of 1948, acts amendatory and supplementary thereto and appropriation acts thereunder, and will make available to the Government of the United Kingdom only such commodities, services, and other assistance as are authorized to be made available by such acts.

(2) The Government of the United Kingdom, acting individually and through the Organization for European Economic Co-operation, consistently with the Convention for European Economic Co-operation signed at Paris on 16 April 1948, will exert sustained efforts in common with other participating countries speedily to achieve through a joint recovery programme economic conditions in Europe essential to lasting peace and prosperity and to enable the countries of Europe participating in such a joint recovery programme to become independent of extraordinary outside economic assistance within the period of this Agreement. The Government of the United Kingdom reaffirms its intention to take action to carry out the provisions of the General Obligations of the Convention for European Economic Co-operation, to continue to participate actively in the work of the Organization for European Economic Co-operation, and to continue to adhere to the purposes and policies of the Economic Co-operation Act of 1948.

(3) With respect to assistance furnished by the Government of the United States of America to the United Kingdom and procured from areas outside the United States of America, its territories and possessions, the Government of the United Kingdom will co-operate with the Government of the United States of America in ensuring that procurement will be effected at reasonable prices and on reasonable terms and so as to arrange that the dollars thereby made available to the country from which the assistance is procured are used in a manner consistent with any arrangements made by the Government of the United States of America with such country.

Article II

(1) In order to achieve the maximum recovery through the employment of assistance received from the Government of the United States of America, the Government of the United Kingdom will use its best endeavours:

(a) To adopt or maintain the measures necessary to ensure efficient and practical use of all the resources available to it including—

   (i) Such measures as may be necessary to ensure that the commodities and services obtained with assistance furnished under this Agreement are used for purposes consistent with this Agreement and, as far as practicable, with the general purposes outlined in the schedules furnished by the Government of the United Kingdom in support of the requirements of assistance to be furnished by the Government of the United States of America;

   (ii) The observation and review of the use of such resources through an effective follow-up system approved by the Organization for European Economic Co-operation; and

   (iii) To the extent practicable, measures to locate, identify, and put into appropriate use in furtherance of the joint programme for European recovery, assets, and earnings therefrom, which belong to nationals of the United Kingdom and which are situated within the United States of America, its territories or possessions; it being understood that nothing in this clause imposes any obligation on the Government of the United States of America to assist in carrying out such measures, or on the Government of the United Kingdom to dispose of such assets;

(b) To promote the development of industrial and agricultural production on a sound economic basis; to achieve such production targets as may be established through the Organization for European Economic Co-operation; and when desired by the Government of the United States of America to communicate to that Government detailed proposals for specific projects contemplated by the Government of the United Kingdom to be undertaken in substantial part with assistance made available pursuant to this Agreement, including whenever practicable projects for increased production of coal, steel, transportation facilities, and food;

(c) To stabilize its currency, establish or maintain a valid rate of exchange, balance its Governmental budget, create or maintain internal financial stability, and generally restore or maintain confidence in its monetary system; and

(d) To co-operate with other participating countries in facilitating and stimulating an increasing interchange of goods and services among the participating countries and with other countries and in reducing public and private barriers to trade among themselves and with other countries.

(2) Taking into account Article 8 of the Convention for European Economic Co-operation, looking toward the full and effective use of manpower available in the participating countries, the Government of the United Kingdom will accord sympathetic consideration to proposals made in conjunction with the International Refugee Organization directed to the largest practicable utilization of manpower available in any of the participating countries in furtherance of the accomplishment of the purposes of this Agreement.

(3) The Government of the United Kingdom will take the measures which it deems appropriate, and will co-operate with other participating countries, to prevent, on the part of private or public commercial enterprises, business practices or business arrangements affecting international trade which restrain competition, limit access to markets or foster monopolistic control whenever such practices or arrangements have the effect of interfering with the achievement of the joint programme of European recovery.

Article III

(1) The two Governments will upon the request of either of them consult respecting projects in the United Kingdom proposed by nationals of the United States of America and with regard to which the Government of the United States of America may appropriately make guarantees of currency transfer under Section 111 (b) (3) of the Economic Co-operation Act of 1948.

(2) The Government of the United Kingdom agrees that if the Government of the United States of America makes payment in United States dollars to any person under such a guaranty, any pounds sterling, or credits in pounds sterling, assigned or transferred to the Government of the United States of America pursuant

99

to that section shall be recognized as property of the Government of the United States of America.

Article IV

(1) The provisions of this Article shall apply only with respect to assistance which may be furnished by the Government of the United States of America on a grant basis.

(2) The Government of the United Kingdom will establish a special account in the Bank of England in the name of the Government of the United Kingdom (hereinafter called the Special Account) and will make deposits in pounds sterling to this account as follows:—

(a) The unencumbered balances of the deposits made by the Government of the United Kingdom pursuant to the Exchange of Notes between the two Governments dated 30 April 1948.

(b) Amounts commensurate with the indicated dollar cost to the Government of the United States of America of commodities, services, and technical information (including any cost of processing, storing, transporting, repairing, or other services incident thereto) made available to the United Kingdom on a grant basis by any means authorized under the Economic Co-operation Act of 1948, less, however, the amount of the deposits made pursuant to the Exchange of Notes referred to in sub-paragraph (a). The Government of the United States of America shall from time to time notify the Government of the United Kingdom of the indicated dollar cost of any such commodities, services, and technical information, and the Government of the United Kingdom will thereupon deposit in the Special Account a commensurate amount of pounds sterling computed at a rate of exchange which shall be the par value agreed at such time with the International Monetary Fund.

The Government of the United Kingdom may at any time make advance deposits in the Special Account which shall be credited against subsequent notifications pursuant to this paragraph.

(3) The Government of the United States of America will from time to time notify the Government of the United Kingdom of its requirements for administrative expenditures in pounds sterling within the United Kingdom incident to operations under the Economic Co-operation Act of 1948, and the Government of the United Kingdom will thereupon make such sums available out of any balances in the Special Account in the manner requested by the Government of the United States of America in the notification.

(4) Five per cent of each deposit made pursuant to this Article in

respect of assistance furnished under authority of the Foreign Aid Appropriation Act, 1949, shall be allocated to the use of the Government of the United States of America for its expenditures in the United Kingdom, and sums made available pursuant to paragraph 3 of this Article shall first be charged to the amounts allocated under this paragraph.

(5) The Government of the United Kingdom will further make such sums of pounds sterling available out of any balances in the Special Account as may be required to cover costs (including port, storage, handling and similar charges) of transportation from any point of entry in the United Kingdom to the consignee's designated point of delivery in the United Kingdom of such relief supplies and packages as are referred to in Article VI.

(6) The Government of the United Kingdom may draw upon any remaining balance in the Special Account for such purposes as may be agreed from time to time with the Government of the United States of America. In considering proposals put forward by the Government of the United Kingdom for drawings from the Special Account, the Government of the United States of America will take into account the need for promoting or maintaining internal monetary and financial stabilization in the United Kingdom and for stimulating productive activity and international trade and the exploration for and development of new sources of wealth within the United Kingdom, including in particular:—

(a) Expenditures upon projects or programmes, including those which are part of a comprehensive programme for the development of the productive capacity of the United Kingdom and the other participating countries, and projects or programmes the external costs of which are being covered by assistance rendered by the Government of the United States of America under the Economic Co-operation Act of 1948 or otherwise, or by loans from the International Bank for Reconstruction and Development;

(b) Expenditures upon the exploration for and development of additional production of materials which may be required in the United States of America because of deficiencies or potential deficiencies in the resources of the United States of America; and

(c) Effective retirement of the national debt, especially debt held by the Central Bank or other banking institutions.

(7) Any unencumbered balance, other than unexpended amounts allocated under paragraph 4 of this Article, remaining in the Special Account on 30 June 1952, shall be disposed of within the United Kingdom for such purposes as may hereafter be agreed between the Governments of the United States of America and the United King-

dom, it being understood that the agreement of the United States of America shall be subject to approval by Act or joint resolution of the Congress of the United States of America.

Article V

(1) The Government of the United Kingdom will facilitate the transfer to the United States of America, for stockpiling or other purposes, of materials originating in the United Kingdom which are required by the United States of America as a result of deficiencies or potential deficiencies in its own resources, upon such reasonable terms of sale, exchange, barter, or otherwise, and in such quantities, and for such period of time, as may be agreed to between the Governments of the United States of America and the United Kingdom after due regard for the reasonable requirements of the United Kingdom for domestic use and commercial export of such materials. The Government of the United Kingdom will take such specific measures as may be necessary to carry out the provisions of this paragraph, including the promotion of the increased production of such materials within the United Kingdom, and the removal of any hindrances to the transfer of such materials to the United States of America. The Government of the United Kingdom will, when so requested by the Government of the United States of America, enter into negotiations for detailed arrangements necessary to carry out the provisions of this paragraph.

(2) Recognizing the principle of equity in respect to the drain upon the natural resources of the United States of America and of the participating countries, the Government of the United Kingdom will, when so requested by the Government of the United States of America, negotiate where applicable (a) a future schedule of minimum availabilities to the United States of America for future purchase and delivery of a fair share of materials originating in the United Kingdom which are required by the United States of America as a result of deficiencies or potential deficiencies in its own resources at world market prices so as to protect the access of United States industry to an equitable share of such materials either in percentages of production or in absolute quantities from the United Kingdom, (b) arrangements providing suitable protection for the right of access for any citizen of the United States of America or any corporation, partnership, or other association created under the laws of the United States of America, or of any State or Territory thereof and substantially beneficially owned by citizens of the United States of America, in the development of such materials on terms of treatment equivalent to those afforded to the nationals of the United Kingdom, and, (c) an agreed schedule of increased production of such materials where practicable in the United Kingdom and

for delivery of an agreed percentage of such increased production to be transferred to the United States of America on a long-term basis in consideration of assistance furnished by the United States of America under this Agreement.

(3) The Government of the United Kingdom, when so requested by the Government of the United States of America, will co-operate, wherever appropriate, to further the objectives of paragraphs 1 and 2 of this Article in respect of materials originating outside the United Kingdom.

Article VI

(1) The Government of the United Kingdom will co-operate with the Government of the United States of America in facilitating and encouraging the promotion and development of travel by citizens of the United States of America to and within participating countries.

(2) The Government of the United Kingdom will, when so desired by the Government of the United States of America, enter into negotiations for agreements (including the provision of duty-free treatment under appropriate safeguards) to facilitate the entry into the United Kingdom of supplies of relief goods donated to or purchased by United States voluntary non-profit relief agencies and of relief packages originating in the United States of America and consigned to individuals residing in the United Kingdom.

Article VII

(1) The two Governments will, upon the request of either of them, consult regarding any matter relating to the application of this Agreement or to operations or arrangements carried out pursuant to this Agreement.

(2) The Government of the United Kingdom will communicate to the Government of the United States of America in a form and at intervals to be indicated by the latter after consultation with the Government of the United Kingdom:

(a) Detailed information of projects, programmes, and measures proposed or adopted by the Government of the United Kingdom to carry out the provisions of this Agreement and of the General Obligations of the Convention for European Economic Co-operation;

(b) Full statements of operations under this Agreement, including a statement of the use of funds, commodities, and services received thereunder, such statements to be made in each calendar quarter;

(c) Information regarding its economy and any other relevant information, necessary to supplement that obtained by the

Government of the United States of America from the Organization for European Economic Co-operation, which the Government of the United States of America may need to determine the nature and scope of operations under the Economic Co-operation Act of 1948, and to evaluate the effectiveness of assistance furnished or contemplated under this Agreement and generally the progress of the joint recovery programme.

(3) The Government of the United Kingdom will assist the Government of the United States of America to obtain the information, relating to the materials originating in the United Kingdom referred to in Article V, which is necessary to the formulation and execution of the arrangements provided for in that Article.

Article VIII

(1) The Governments of the United States of America and the United Kingdom recognize that it is in their mutual interest that full publicity be given to the objectives and progress of the joint programme for European recovery and of the actions taken in furtherance of that programme, and that wide dissemination of information on the progress of the programme is desirable in order to develop the sense of common effort and mutual aid which are essential to the accomplishment of the objectives of the programme.

(2) The Government of the United States of America will encourage the dissemination of such information and will make it available to the media of public information.

(3) The Government of the United Kingdom will encourage the dissemination of such information both directly and in co-operation with the Organization for European Economic Co-operation. It will make such information available to the media of public information and take all practicable steps to ensure that appropriate facilities are provided for such dissemination. It will further provide other participating countries and the Organization for European Economic Co-operation with full information on the progress of the programme for economic recovery.

(4) The Government of the United Kingdom will make public in the United Kingdom in each calendar quarter, full statements of operations under this Agreement, including information as to the use of funds, commodities, and services received.

Article IX

(1) The Government of the United Kingdom agrees to receive a Special Mission for Economic Co-operation which will discharge the responsibilities of the Government of the United

States of America in the United Kingdom under this Agreement.

(2) The Government of the United Kingdom will, upon appropriate notification from the Ambassador of the United States of America in the United Kingdom, consider the Special Mission and its personnel, and the United States Special Representative in Europe, as part of the Embassy of the United States of America in the United Kingdom for the purpose of enjoying the privileges and immunities accorded to that Embassy and its personnel of comparable rank. The Government of the United Kingdom will further accord appropriate courtesies to the members and staff of the Joint Committee on Foreign Economic Co-operation of the Congress of the United States of America, and grant them the facilities and assistance necessary to the effective performance of their responsibilities.

(3) The Government of the United Kingdom, directly and through its representatives on the Organization for European Economic Co-operation, will extend full co-operation to the Special Mission, to the United States Special Representative in Europe and his staff, and to the members and staff of the Joint Committee. Such co-operation shall include the provision of all information and facilities necessary to the observation and review of the carrying out of this Agreement, including the use of assistance furnished under it.

Article X

(1) The Governments of the United States of America and the United Kingdom agree to submit to the decision of the International Court of Justice any claim espoused by either Government on behalf of one of its nationals against the other Government for compensaion for damage arising as a consequence of governmental measures (other than measures concerning enemy property or interests) taken after 3 April 1948, by the other Government and affecting the property or interest of such national, including contracts with or concessions granted by duly authorized authorities of such other Government. It is understood that the undertaking of each Government in respect of claims espoused by the other Government pursuant to this paragraph is made in the case of each Government under the authority of, and is limited by, the terms and conditions of its declaration accepting the compulsory jurisdiction of the International Court of Justice under Article 36 of the Statute of the Court, and shall remain in force as to each Government on a basis of reciprocity until 14 August 1951, and thereafter for such period as the declarations of such acceptance by both Governments are in effect, but not later than the date of termination of this Agreement. The provisions of this paragraph shall be in all respects without prejudice

to other rights of access, if any, of either Government to the International Court of Justice or to the espousal and presentation of claims based upon alleged violations by either Government of rights and duties arising under treaties, agreements or principles of international law.

(2) The Governments of the United States of America and the United Kingdom further agree that such claims may be referred, in lieu of the Court, to any arbitral tribunal mutually agreed upon.

(3) It is further understood that neither Government will espouse a claim pursuant to this Article until its national has exhausted the remedies available to him in the administrative and judicial tribunals of the country in which the claim arose.

Article XI

As used in this agreement:—

(a) 'The United Kingdom' means the United Kingdom of Great Britain and Northern Ireland and any territory to which this Agreement shall have been extended under the provisions of Article XII.

(b) The term 'participating country' means (i) any country which signed the Report of the Committee of European Co-operation at Paris on 22 September 1947, and any territories for which it has international responsibility and to which the Economic Co-operation Agreement concluded between that country and the Government of the United States of America has been applied, and (ii) any other country (including any of the zones of occupation of Germany, and areas under international administration or control, and the Free Territory of Trieste or either of its zones) wholly or partly in Europe, together with dependent areas under its administration; provided that, and for so long as, such country is a party to the Convention for European Economic Co-operation and adheres to a joint programme for European recovery designed to accomplish the purposes of this Agreement.

(c) The expression 'nationals of the United Kingdom' shall mean British subjects belonging to, and companies and associations incorporated under the laws of, the United Kingdom or any territory to which this Agreement shall have been extended under Article XII.

Article XII

This Agreement shall, on the part of the Government of the United Kingdom, extend to the United Kingdom of Great Britain and Northern Ireland, to the territories specified in the schedule attached hereto, and to any other territories (being territories for whose international relations the Government of the United Kingdom is responsible) from the date on which the Government of the United Kingdom notifies the Government of the United States of America of the extension of the Agreement to them. Nothing in the Agreement shall be construed as imposing any obligation contrary to the terms of a Trusteeship Agreement in force in relation to any territory.

SCHEDULE

Aden
Bahamas
Cyprus
Falkland Islands
Fiji and Western Pacific High Commission territories (excluding Tonga and New Hebrides)
Gambia
Gibraltar
Gold Coast
Hong Kong
Kenya
Malta
Mauritius
Nigeria
Nyasaland
St Helena and Dependencies
Seychelles
Sierra Leone
Singapore
Tanganyika
Uganda
Windward Islands
Zanzibar

Article XIII

(1) This Agreement shall become effective on this day's date. Subject to the provisions of paragraphs 2 and 3 of this Article, it shall remain in force until 30 June 1953, and, unless at least six months before 30 June 1953, either Government shall have given notice in writing to the other of intention to terminate the Agreement on that date it shall remain in force thereafter until the expiration of six months from the date on which such notice shall have been given.

(2) If, during the life of this Agreement, either Government should consider there has been a fundamental change in the basic assumptions underlying the Agreement, it shall so notify the other Government in writing and the two Governments will thereupon consult with a view to agreeing upon the amendment, modification or termination of the Agreement. If, after three months from such notification, the two Governments have not agreed upon the action to be taken in the circumstances, either Government may give notice in writing to the other of intention to terminate the Agreement. Subject to the provisions of paragraph 3 of this Article, the Agreement shall then terminate either—

(a) Six months after the date of such notice of intention to terminate, or

(b) After such shorter period as may be agreed to be sufficient to ensure that the obligations of the Government of the United Kingdom are performed in respect of any assistance which may continue to be furnished by the Government of the United States of America after the date of such notice; provided, however, that Article V and paragraph 3 of Article VII shall remain in effect until two years after the date of such notice of intention to terminate, but not later than 30 June 1953.

(3) Subsidiary agreements and arrangements negotiated pursuant to this Agreement may remain in force beyond the date of termination of the Agreement and the period of effectiveness of such subsidiary agreements and arrangements shall be governed by their own terms. Article IV shall remain in effect until all the sums in pounds sterling required to be deposited in accordance with its terms have been disposed of as provided in that Article. Paragraph 2 of Article III shall remain in effect for so long as the guarantee payments referred to in that Article may be made by the Government of the United States of America.

(4) This Agreement may be amended at any time by agreement between the two Governments.

(5) The Annex to this Agreement forms an integral part thereof.

(6) This Agreement shall be registered with the Secretary-General of the United Nations.

IN WITNESS whereof the respective representatives, duly authorized for the purpose, have signed the present Agreement.

Done in London, in duplicate, this sixth day of July 1948.

(Sd.)   ERNEST BEVIN
(Sd.)   LEWIS W. DOUGLAS

ANNEX

INTERPRETATIVE NOTES

It is understood that the requirements of paragraph 1 (a) of Article II relating to the adoption of measures for the efficient use of resources, would include, with respect to commodities furnished under the Agreement, effective measures for safeguarding such commodities and for preventing their diversion to illegal or irregular markets or channels of trade.

(2) It is understood that the obligation under paragraph 1 (c) of Article II to balance the budget would not preclude deficits over a short period but would mean a budgetary policy involving the balancing of the budget in the long run.

(3) It is understood that the business practices and business arrangements referred to in paragraph 3 of Article II mean—

(a) Fixing prices, terms, or conditions to be observed in dealing with others in the purchase, sale, or lease of any product;

(b) Excluding enterprises from, or allocating or dividing, any territorial market or field of business activity, or allocating customers, or fixing sales quotas or purchase quotas;

(c) Discriminating against particular enterprises;

(d) Limiting production or fixing production quotas;

(e) Preventing by agreement the development or application of technology or invention whether patented or unpatented;

(f) Extending the use of rights under patents, trade marks, or copyrights granted by either country to matters which, according to its laws and regulations, are not within the scope of such grants, or to products or conditions of production, use, or sale which are likewise not the subjects of such grants; and

(g) Such other practices as the two Governments may agree to include.

(4) It is understood that the Government of the United Kingdom is obligated to take action in particular instances in accordance with paragraph 3 of Article II only after appropriate investigation or examination.

(5) It is understood that the phrase in Article V 'after due regard for the reasonable requirements of the United Kingdom for domestic use' would include the maintenance of reasonable stocks of the materials concerned and that the phrase 'commercial export' might include barter transactions. It is also understood that arrangements negotiated under Article V might appropriately include provision for consultation, in accordance with the principles of Article 32 of the Havana Charter for an International Trade Organization, in the event that stockpiles are liquidated.

(6) It is understood that it should not be assumed from paragraph 2 of Article VI that the existing facilities extended by the United Kingdom to relief goods and packages are inadequate.

(7) It is understood that the Government of the United Kingdom will not be requested, under paragraph 2 (a) of Article VII, to furnish detailed information about minor projects or confidential commercial or technical information the disclosure of which would injure legitimate commercial interests.

(8) It is understood that the Government of the United States of America in making the notifications referred to in paragraph 2 of Article IX would bear in mind the desirability of restricting, so far as practicable, the number of officials for whom full diplomatic privileges would be requested. It is also understood that the detailed application of Article IX would, when necessary, be the subject of inter-Governmental discussion.

(9) It is understood that any agreements which might be arrived

at pursuant to paragraph 2 of Article X would be subject to ratification by the Senate of the United States of America.

NOTE

His Majesty's Principal Secretary of State for Foreign Affairs to His Excellency the United States Ambassador

London,
Your Excellency,   6 *July 1948*.

I have the honour to draw your attention to the fact that it is impossible for the United Kingdom Government, on signing the Economic Co-operation Agreement with the Government of the United States, to give a complete list of those Colonial territories which will participate in the Agreement. The reason is that in several cases it is necessary for Colonial Governments to be given a reasonable opportunity of considering the implications of the Agreement for them.

I have also explained to your Excellency that a decision in the case of Southern Rhodesia will rest entirely with the Government of that country, and that the Government of the United Kingdom is unable at this time to say what the decision will be.

It is my understanding that most Colonial Governments may be expected to participate in the Agreement within a very short time. But the Government of the United Kingdom recognizes that if within a reasonable period after the signature of the Agreement some of the more important territories concerned (other than Southern Rhodesia) are not participating in it the Government of the United States would be entitled to regard this as a change in the relationship of the parties under the Agreement, affecting the form or continuance of assistance to the United Kingdom. It is my understanding that before any action were to be taken by the Government of the United States there would be consultation between the two Governments.

I have, &c.
(Sd.)   ERNEST BEVIN

AGREEMENT FOR INTRA-EUROPEAN PAYMENTS AND COMPENSATIONS[1]

Paris, 16 October 1948

The Governments of Austria, Belgium, Denmark, France, Greece, Ireland, Iceland, Italy, Luxembourg, Norway, the Netherlands, Portugal, the United Kingdom, Sweden, Switzerland, and Turkey, the Commanders-in-Chief of the French, United Kingdom, and United States Zones of Occupation of Germany, and the Commander of the British-United States Zone of the Free Territory of Trieste:

Desiring to move forward towards the liberalization of Intra-European Payments envisaged in Article 4 of the Convention for European Economic Co-operation signed in Paris on 16 April 1948.[2]

Desiring to adopt immediately a plan for limited compensation to be applied until it shall be possible to take further steps towards the establishment of a full multilateral system of payments among themselves;

Having regard to the adoption on 16 October 1948, by the Council of the Organization for European Economic Co-operation (hereinafter referred to as the Council) of a Decision approving the text of the present Agreement; and to the adoption on 16 October 1948, of a Decision recommending a distribution of American Aid;

Considering the Decision on commercial policy taken by the Council on 16 October 1948;

Have agreed as follows:

PART I

Article 1

(a) Subject to the provisions of the present Agreement, the Contracting Parties shall carry out currency compensations. Such compensations shall be first and second category compensations as defined in Article 18. Compensations shall be used to facilitate all transactions which the Contracting Parties may at any time allow in accordance with their respective transfer policies and with the terms of their payments agreements.

(b) Subject to the provisions of Article 5, the balances available for compensations shall be the balances of accounts kept by one

[1] Cmd. 7546.
[2] 'Miscellaneous No. 4 (1948),' Cmd. 7388.

central bank in the name of other central banks. For the purposes of the present Agreement, central banks shall be the central banks or other monetary authorities designated by the Contracting Parties.

Article 2

The Bank for International Settlements (hereinafter referred to as the Agent), acting in accordance with the agreement between the Bank for International Settlements and the Organization for European Economic Co-operation (hereinafter referred to as the Organization) made in pursuance of the Decision of the Council taken on 10 September 1948, shall be the Agent for compensation for the purposes of the present Agreement.

Article 3

(a) Compensations under the present Agreement shall take place monthly and in accordance with directives given by the Organization to the Agent.

(b) The Agent shall submit monthly reports to the Organization on the compensations completed during the month.

Article 4

(a) First category compensations shall be applied without the previous consent of the Contracting Parties.

(b) Second category compensations shall require the previous consent of the Contracting Parties directly concerned in each second category compensation.

(c) The Contracting Parties, while not binding themselves to accept second category compensations, intend to co-operate fully in facilitating any reasonable propositions put forward to them by the Agent, having regard to all the circumstances concerning such compensations.

(d) In arranging second category compensations the Agent shall endeavour to facilitate those compensations which will ease the most difficult debtor/creditor relationships, bearing particularly in mind the desirability of avoiding so far as possible settlements between Contracting Parties in gold or foreign currencies and interruptions in trade or payments.

(e) Nothing in this Article shall prevent any Contracting Party from informing the Agent that it is prepared to accept, without its previous consent, all or any class of second category compensations which may be arranged by the Agent.

Article 5

(a) When calculating the balances available for the compensations in respect of any month, the Agent, at the request of a Contracting Party, may exclude certain types of balances owned by that Contracting Party. The types of balances which may be excluded and the procedure for requesting their exclusion are set out in Annex A which shall form an integral part of the present Agreement.

(b) No balance excluded under paragraph (a) of this Article from the compensations in respect of any month shall be included, by the Contracting Party requesting the exclusion, in the calculation for the purpose of any settlement in gold or foreign currency which would be due to that Contracting Party under a payments agreement made before the signature of the present Agreement and which might follow immediately after the compensations in respect of that month.

Article 6

Each Contracting Party undertakes not to cause abnormal balances in the currencies of other Contracting Parties to be held by banks other than central banks or otherwise to place such balances so that they will not be available for the purpose of compensations.

Article 7

(a) Whenever a gold or foreign currency settlement falls due in the course of any month, under a payments agreement between any two Contracting Parties made before the signature of the present Agreement, the settlement shall be postponed until after the compensations in respect of that month.

(b) Any settlement in gold or foreign currency which shall remain due after the compensations in respect of that month shall then be effected immediately. Any such settlement shall be reported by the debtor to the Agent and the Organization.

(c) Nothing in the provisions of this Article shall preclude a Contracting Party which is a creditor from making different provisions by agreement with another Contracting Party, if, owing to the operation of this Article, a credit margin granted by the former to the latter is being continuously exceeded.

Article 8

(a) Each Contracting Party shall communicate to the Agent:

(i) All information necessary to enable the Agent to have a clear understanding of the nature and operation of its payments agreements with other Contracting Parties;

(ii) A monthly statement of the balances on the appropriate account or accounts available for compensations, and of the balances which the Contracting Party desires to exclude in accordance with Article 5;

(iii) A monthly report giving a single rate of exchange agreed

113

with each other Contracting Party at which the Contracting Party reporting is prepared for compensations to take place;

(iv) A monthly statement of settlements in gold or foreign currency made by the Contracting Party to other Contracting Parties during the month;

(v) Such information as will enable the Agent to ascertain the amounts of currencies which may be used in accordance with Part II of the present Agreement; and

(vi) Such further information as the Contracting Party considers may assist the Agent in his task.

(b) In the case of Contracting Parties without a unified cross-rate structure, the balances and rates of exchange reported under sub-paragraphs (ii) and (iii) of paragraph (a) of this Article, shall be determined in accordance with the provisions of Annex B which shall form an integral part of the present Agreement.

PART II

Article 9

(a) Each Contracting Party which has for the purpose of the present Agreement been estimated to be in credit with any other Contracting Party on current balance of payments for the year ending 30 June 1949, after taking into account the agreed existing resources of that other Contracting Party, shall establish drawing rights in favour of the latter Contracting Party.

(b) The amounts of drawing rights established by each creditor in favour of each debtor, equivalent to the United States dollar value of goods and services to be provided by the United States Economic Co-operation Administration for the purposes of the present Agreement (hereinafter referred to as conditional aid) to each creditor, are shown in Annex C which shall form an integral part of the present Agreement.

(c) No debtor shall be obliged to repay to a creditor any amount in respect of drawing rights established by the creditor in its favour, if that creditor has received from the United States Economic Co-operation Administration an equivalent amount of conditional aid to which no obligation to repay is attached.

(d) For the purposes of this Part of the present Agreement 'creditor' and 'debtor' mean, with respect to any two Contracting Parties, those which are shown as creditor and debtor in relation to one another in Table III of Annex C.

Article 10

Drawing rights shall be made available and used only in accordance with the provisions of the present Agreement. The amount to be made available and used shall be calculated in accordance with the provisions of Annex B.

Article 11

(a) Subject to the provisions of paragraph (b) of this Article, drawing rights shall be made available in the currency of the Contracting Party making them available, or, if another currency is normally used for payments between that Contracting Party and another Contracting Party, in that other currency. Each Contracting Party shall, not later than 31 October 1948, report to the Agent the currencies in which it will make drawing rights available in accordance with this paragraph.

(b) Any two Contracting Parties may agree, not later than 31 October 1948, that the drawing rights established by one in favour of the other shall be made available in a currency different from the currency in which they would otherwise be made available under paragraph (a) of this Article. A report on any such agreement shall be given by the two Contracting Parties to the Agent not later than 31 October 1948.

(c) An agreement between two Contracting Parties under paragraph (b) of this Article shall not prevent them from subsequently making an agreement that the drawing rights established by one in favour of the other shall be made available either in the currency of one of them or in a currency which, at the time of the subsequent agreement, is normally used for payments between them. Immediately after any such subsequent agreement, the two Contracting Parties shall make a report thereon to the Agent.

Article 12

Amounts of currency in respect of drawing rights shall be made available to the Agent immediately upon request by him, provided that a Contracting Party shall not be required to make amounts of currency available to the Agent earlier than the time at which equivalent amounts of conditional aid are firmly allotted to it.

Article 13

Requests under Article 12 in respect of the drawing rights established in favour of any Contracting Party in any currency shall not be made before the agreed existing resources of that Contracting Party in that currency, as set out in Annex C, have been exhausted.

Article 14

The Agent shall use amounts of currencies made available under this Part of the present Agreement in compensations under the present Agreement in accordance with the following provisions:

(*a*) (i) The Agent shall be entitled to use in any month an amount of any one currency up to the total of each deficit on the month between each debtor and each creditor to the extent to which the remaining amount of agreed existing resources of that debtor in that currency is not sufficient to cover that deficit.

(ii) If in any month an amount of such currency is not made available as a result of the operation of Article 12, the whole or part of that amount, when it becomes available, may be used by the Agent in any succeeding month in addition to the amount which he may use under sub-paragraph (i) of this paragraph.

(*b*) The Agent may, at the request of a debtor, use all or any part of amounts of a particular currency, additional to those which might be used under paragraph (*a*) of this Article, as the debtor may intimate to him, provided that:

(i) any Contracting Party, whose monthly deficit against the Contracting Party by which the drawing right has been established in favour of the debtor is to be reduced by the use of the amount, has no balance standing to his credit with the Contracting Party which has established the drawing right, or

(ii) the consent of the Contracting Party by which the drawing right has been established has first been obtained.

(*c*) If in any month the aggregate amount of any one currency which the Agent is entitled to use under sub-paragraph (*a*) of this Article exceeds the amount of such currency available under this Part of the present Agreement, the Agent shall, in principle, use such currency as between the Contracting Parties in deficit on the month in that currency in proportion to such deficits, but may make moderate adjustments in this proportionate distribution having regard to the desirability of creating a minimum of interruption in trade and payments and of assisting in the avoidance of gold and foreign currency settlements.

Article 15

Not more than 75 per cent of the amount of drawing rights established by a Contracting Party in favour of another Contracting Party as shown in Annex C shall be made available and used in compensations in respect of the nine months ending 31 March 1949. In particular cases this percentage may be increased by decision of the Organization.

Article 16

(*a*) If a Contracting Party, either under a payments agreement or because it has no available credit balance in the currency of another Contracting Party, has made a payment in gold or foreign currency falling due on or after 1 October 1948 to that other Contracting Party because at the time of payment drawing rights established in its favour by that other Contracting Party could not be used by the Agent as a result of the operation of the provisions of Articles 12 and 15, the Agent, at the request of the Contracting Party which has made the payment, shall take the necessary steps to enable such drawing rights to be used to repurchase the whole or part of any amounts of gold or foreign currency so paid provided that the use of the drawing rights is no longer prevented as a result of the operation of the provisions of Articles 12 and 15.

(b) The request and arrangements under paragraph (a) of this Article shall be made and put into effect during the course of the compensations in respect of the month when the provisions of Articles 12 and 15, as the case may be, cease to prevent the use of the drawing rights.

(c) The amount which the Agent may use under this Article in respect of any month shall be in addition to the amounts which the Agent may use in respect of that month under Article 14.

Article 17

(a) It is contemplated that drawing rights will normally be used as established under Article 9 of the present Agreement. The procedure for revisions provided for in paragraphs (b), (c), and (d) of this Article shall be administered with this in mind.

(b) Revision of the amounts and distribution of drawing rights shall take place, at the request of a Contracting Party, only in circumstances resulting from:

(i) *force majeure* or catastrophe;

(ii) a situation in which a debtor maintains and satisfies the Council that it has been unable to use the whole or any part of its drawing rights although it has made all reasonable efforts to do so; or

(iii) a situation in which a creditor maintains and satisfies the Council that the whole or any part of drawing rights established by it are no longer required by a debtor for the purposes for which they were established.

(c) The Council shall establish appropriate bodies to deal with cases arising under this Article.

(d) The Council shall decide what recommendations for revision of the amounts of and for the redistribution of drawing rights should be made to the United States Economic Co-operation Administration.

PART III

Article 18

(a) 'First category compensation' means an operation which produces for any Contracting Party all or any of the following results:

(i) a decrease in one or more debit balances against an equivalent decrease in one or more credit balances, or

(ii) the off-setting, by the use of amounts in respect of drawing rights established in its favour, of the whole or part of its deficit for the month with the Contracting Party by which the drawing rights have been established, or, in the case of amounts which may be used under Article 14 (*a*) (ii), the off-setting of the whole or part of a deficit with that Contracting Party remaining uncovered from a previous month or months,

provided that amounts in respect of drawing rights shall, to the extent to which they are not used to off-set deficits under sub-paragraph (ii) of this paragraph, be treated for the purposes of sub-paragraph (i) as if they were credit balances.

(b) 'Second category compensation' means any operation, other than one included under paragraph (*a*) of this Article, which results in the increase of a balance or the formation of a new balance in comparison with tee position before the operation.

Article 19

If a Contracting Party in placing information at the disposal of the Agent for the purposes of the present Agreement intimates that it desires the information to be treated as confidential, because the information has not been published by it, the Agent shall have due regard to the intimation in making use of the information.

Article 20

(*a*) Any compensation which requires the use of the balance of any account kept by or in the name of the central bank of Portugal or Switzerland shall be subject to the previous consent of Portugal or Switzerland and the respective creditor or debtor.

(*b*) Subject to approval by the Council, the Government of Portugal or the Government of Switzerland may, at any time, decide to accept without their previous consent all first category compensations. Upon such approval, the provisions of paragraph (*a*) of this Article shall cease to apply to Portugal or to Switzerland, as the case may be, and to their respective creditors and debtors.

(*c*) Part II of the present Agreement shall not apply to Portugal or to Switzerland.

Article 21

If a special Agreement is made between any Contracting Party and the United States Economic Co-operation Administration with respect to the payment or loan of United States dollars to any such Contracting Party for the purposes of the present Agreement, Part II of the present Agreement shall operate in relation to that Contracting Party upon such conditions regarding its application for the purposes of the present Agreement as may be proposed by that Contracting Party in agreement with the United States Economic Co-operation Administration and approved by the Council. The conditions will, upon approval by the Council, be communicated by the Secretary-General to the Agent.

Article 22

(a) The supervision of the operation of the present Agreement shall be undertaken by the Organization.

(b) Should any question arise concerning the interpretation or the application of the present Agreement, it may be referred by any Contracting Party to the Council which may take decisions on the question.

Article 23

(a) The present Agreement shall be ratified.

(b) The instruments of ratification shall be deposited with the Secretary-General of the Organization who will notify each deposit to all the signatories.

(c) The present Agreement shall come into force upon the deposit of instruments of ratification by all the signatories.

Article 24

(a) Drawing rights not used before the termination of the present Agreement shall not be cancelled. They will remain at the disposal of the Contracting Parties in whose favour they have been established under no less favourable terms than those originally enjoyed.

(b) The precise method by which such unused drawing rights shall be disposed of in the period subsequent to the termination of the Agreement shall be the subject of discussion by the Organization at the appropriate time.

Article 25

(a) With the exception of Article 24, the present Agreement shall remain in force until the completion of the compensations in respect of the month of June 1949, and the present Agreement may be continued in force thereafter on such terms as the Contracting Parties may agree. Article 24 shall remain in force until the unused drawing rights have been finally disposed of.

(b) Not later than 1 May 1949, the Contracting Parties, acting through the Organization, shall consider how the present Agreement has worked and whether it shall be continued.

(c) If it becomes apparent that the present Agreement is not likely to be continued in force, the Contracting Parties shall, at the request of any Contracting Party, entrust a Committee or Committees with the preparation of recommendations as to the provisions which may be required to avoid,

(i) interruptions in trade or payments,

(ii) payments of gold or foreign currency,

(iii) the prevention of repurchase of gold or foreign currency which would otherwise have been possible under the provisions of the present Agreement, or

(iv) other similar possible consequences,

which may arise, within a reasonable time from the termination of the present Agreement, as a result of changes in balances caused by compensations made under the present Agreement.

Article 26

The present Agreement terminates the First Agreement for Multilateral Monetary Compensation, signed in Paris on 18 November 1947, as from the completion of the compensations in respect of the month of September, 1948.

ANNEX A

EXCLUDED BALANCES

I. The following balances may be excluded from compensations under Article 5 of the present Agreement:

(*a*) Working balances, which will normally fall under one or more of the following heads;

(i) normal central banking balances (*fonds de roulement*), that is to say, sufficient funds to cover outstanding payment orders and to maintain normal banking relationships,

(ii) balances held as cover for oversold forward exchange positions, or

(iii) balances held as cover for banking credits due to mature within a short period.

(*b*) Balances representing the proceeds of capital transactions expressly undertaken for the financing of specific capital expenditure.

(*c*) Balances not arising under a payments agreement or from current trade transactions and which are freely convertible into gold or United States dollars.

(*d*) Other balances which, owing to special provisions in payments agreements in force at the date of signature of the present Agreement, represent the proceeds of certain exports earmarked for debt services or other contractual obligations.

(*e*) In the case of Greece and Turkey, in view of the essentially agricultural structure of their economies, a reasonable proportion of their balances in the currencies of other Contracting Parties with which they have no payments agreements providing for credit margins in their favour, it being understood that these balances would be used, during the year following the date of their first exclusion, to pay for imports from the countries in which the balances are held.

II. (*a*) Each Contracting Party requesting the exclusion, under any of the foregoing provisions of this Annex, of a balance owned by it shall state to the Agent the provisions of this Annex under which each reservation is requested and give information as to the facts in reasonable detail.

(*b*) If the Agent is unable to satisfy himself with regard to the requested exclusion from the information given him, he may seek further information.

(*c*) If he remains unsatisfied, he shall make a report on the matter to the Organization and shall furnish a copy of such report to the Contracting Party making the request.

ANNEX B

I. The following procedure shall be used in determining the balances and rates of exchange for the purpose of reports under Article 8 by Contracting Parties without a unified cross rate structure:

(*a*) Debit and credit balances in the currency of any Contracting Party without a unified cross rate structure in relation to Contracting Parties having a unified cross rate structure shall be reported to the Agent in the currency of the latter Contracting Parties, after having been calculated at a rate of exchange to be fixed by agreement between the two Contracting Parties concerned. The rate of exchange so agreed should be that effectively in use for current operations between them. If there are variable rates, or more than one rate, the rate agreed should be based on the weighted average of those rates.

(*b*) The debit and credit balances between each pair of Contracting Parties not having a unified cross rate structure, unless expressed in the currency of a Contracting Party having a unified cross rate structure, shall be reported to the Agent in the money of account used for compensations by him, after having been calculated at a rate of exchange agreed between the two Contracting Parties.

(*c*) The Contracting Party shall also report to the Agent the method of calculation of the reported balances including the data necessary to show how the rates of exchange have been determined for the purpose of their calculation.

II. The following procedure shall be used for the purpose of calculating monthly deficits and of determining the amounts in respect of drawing rights to be made available and used in each month:

(*a*) The Agent shall establish the net balances existing between Contracting Parties and shall convert such net balances into the money of account on the basis of the rates already reported to him. The Agent will then be able to ascertain, in the money of account, the monthly deficits and surpluses and the amounts of drawing rights to be made available and used in each month.

(*b*) In the event of the rate of exchange of the currency of any Contracting Party changing, the Contracting Parties concerned shall advise the Agent of the balances held between them as at the close of business on the day preceding the change and give details of any adjusting payments which may have been made in accordance with the terms of exchange guarantees. The Contracting Parties concerned shall also forward to the Agent a report in accordance with the terms of Article 8 (*a*) (iii) of the Agreement giving the new agreed rate of exchange.

This information will enable the Agent to make allowance for the change in the rate of exchange when calculating the monthly deficits and surpluses and also the amount of drawing rights to be made available.

III. In order to give effect to the compensations in respect of any month, including the use of amounts in respect of drawing rights, the figures notified by the Agent to the Contracting Parties in the currency of Contracting Parties having a unified cross rate structure or in the money of account shall be converted by the Contracting Parties, if necessary, in the currencies of Contracting Parties without a unified cross rate structure on the basis of the rates agreed in accordance with paragraph I of this Annex.

ANNEX C

TABLE I

AGREED EXISTING RESOURCES

The following table sets out the amounts of the agreed existing resources referred to in Article 13 of the present Agreement.

Contracting Parties	Amount of the agreed existing resources (Figures in millions)	Contracting Parties in whose currency the agreed existing resources are held	Dollar equivalent of the amounts of agreed existing resources, calculated prior to the signature of the present Agreement (Figures in millions)
Greece	3·23 £ sterling	United Kingdom	13
Italy	11·16 £ sterling	United Kingdom	45
Bizone	35·22 Swedish crowns	Sweden	9,8
Total ..	14·39 £ sterling		58
Total	35·22 Swedish crowns		9,8
Grand total ..			67,8

TABLE II

DRAWING RIGHTS

(a) Column 2 of the table sets out the total amount of drawing rights established under Article 9 of the present Agreement by each Contracting Party which has been estimated to be in credit with any other Contracting Party on current balance of payments for the year ending 30 June 1949, after taking into account the agreed existing resources of that other Contracting Party.

(b) Column 3 sets out the corresponding total amount of drawing rights established in favour of each Contracting Party.

(c) The amounts specified in this table and in table III are subject to adjustment as follows:

(i) From the amount of the respective drawing rights established by any Contracting Party there shall be deducted the amount of the advance allotments authorized in respect of the third quarter of 1948 by the United States Economic Co-operation Administration under the Economic Co-operation Act of 1948 for the payment for commodities sold by that Contracting Party to any other Contracting Party;

Column 1	Column 2	Column 3
Contracting Parties	Total amounts of drawing rights established by the Contracting Parties named in column 1 in favour of other Contracting Parties	Total amount of drawing rights established in favour of the Contracting Parties named in column 1 by the other Contracting Parties
	Equivalent in United States Dollars (Figures in millions)	Equivalent in United States Dollars (Figures in millions)
Austria	3,1	66,6
Belgium-Luxembourg ..	218·5	11,0
Denmark	5,1	11,9
France	9,7	333
Greece	,,	66,8
Italy	47,3	27
Netherlands	11,3	83
Norway	16,5	48,3
Sweden	34,8	9,8
Turkey	28·5	8,8
United Kingdom	312	30
Bizone	108,8	98,6
French Zone	14,8	15,6
	810,4	810,4

NOTE.—The figures inserted for the United Kingdom cover also the countries (including Iceland and Ireland) which comprise the sterling area, that is to say, the 'Scheduled Territories' as defined for exchange control purposes in United Kingdom legislation.

(ii) From the amount of the respective drawing rights established in favour of any Contracting Party there shall be deducted the
amount of such advance allotments auhtorized in respect of the
third quarter of 1948 for the payment for commodities purchased
by that Contracting Party from any other Contracting Party.

The Secretary-General of the Organization will ask the United
States Economic Co-operation Administration to inform him of the
amounts of the advance allotments mentioned in sub-paragraphs (i)
and (ii) of this paragraph. The Secretary-General will submit to the
Council for approval the amounts adjusted in accordance with sub-
paragraphs (i) and (ii) of this paragraph. Upon approval by the
Council, these amounts shall be substituted for the corresponding
amounts shown in this table and in table III and shall be forwarded
by the Secretary-General to the Agent not later than 31 October
1948.

(*d*) Subject to approval by the United States Economic Co-
operation Administration and by the Council, the respective amounts
of drawing rights may be further adjusted to the extent to which a
Contracting Party has been unable to use any advance allotment.

The Government of Turkey, while approving the terms of the
present Agreement, reserves its position as to the accuracy of the
figures shown in the Annex C relating to Turkey and will, as soon
as possible, make every effort, under the aegis of the Organization,
to reach agreement with the countries concerned on the adjustment
of these figures.

In witness whereof, the undersigned Plenipotentiaries, duly empowered, have appended their signatures to the present Agreement.

Done in Paris this sixteenth day of October, Nineteen Hundred
and Forty-eight, in the English and French languages, both texts
being equally authentic, in a single copy which shall remain
deposited with the Secretary-General of the Organization for
European Economic Co-operation by which certified copies shall
be communicated to all the signatories.

[*Here follow the Signatures*]

N.B.: Ireland signed subject to the following reservation:—

As Ireland has no payments agreements with other countries and
is a member of the sterling area the provisions of the present Agreement require no specific action by her and signature of the present
Agreement on her behalf is subject to the understanding that its
operation will not modify the existing arrangements governing
payments between her and the other Contracting Parties.

TABLE III

DETAILS OF DRAWING RIGHTS

(a) The following table sets out in detail the distribution as between each pair of Contracting Parties of the amounts of drawing rights set out in Table II.

(b) It also shows the pairs of Contracting Parties which are, for the purpose of Part II of the present Agreement, creditors and debtors in relation to one another, as indicated by the figures in the lines opposite and columns under their names.

All figures in millions of dollars

Contracting Parties by which amounts of drawing rights shown are established (Creditors)	Contracting Parties in favour of which amounts of drawing rights shown are established (Debtors)													Total amount of drawing rights established by Contracting Parties
	Austria	Belgium, Luxembourg	Denmark	France	Greece	Italy	Netherlands	Norway	Sweden	Turkey	United Kingdom	Bizone	French Zone	
Austria	—	—	—	—	0,4	2,0	—	—	0,7	—	—	—	—	3,1
Belgium, Luxembourg	4,5	—	6,5	40,0	13,0	—	72,5	23,0	6,0	2,0	30,0	17,0	4,0	218,5
Denmark	0,1	—	—	—	2,0	—	—	—	3,0	—	—	—	—	5,1
France	2,0	—	2,7	—	5,0	—	—	—	—	—	—	—	—	9,7
Greece	—	—	—	—	—	—	—	—	—	—	—	—	—	—
Italy	1,0	11,0	—	11,0	7,0	—	—	0,5	0,1	5,0	—	10,1	2,6	47,3
Netherlands	1,5	—	—	—	5,0	—	—	2,5	—	0,8	—	—	2,0	11,3
Norway	—	—	—	5,0	2,0	—	—	—	—	1,0	—	5,0	—	16,5
Sweden	—	—	—	—	5,0	—	—	21,8	—	—	—	8,0	—	34,8
Turkey	—	—	1,5	—	13,0	—	2,0	—	—	—	—	12,0	—	28,5
United Kingdom	25,0	—	—	200,0	10,0	25,0	—	—	—	—	—	46,5	5,5	312
Bizone	32,0	—	1,0	63,0	4,3	—	8,5	—	—	—	—	—	—	108,8
French Zone	0,5	—	0,2	14,0	0,1	—	—	—	—	—	—	—	—	14,8
Total amounts of drawing rights established in favour of contracting parties	66,6	11,0	11,9	333,0	66,8	27,0	83,0	48,3	9,8	8,8	30,0	98,6	15,6	810,4

NOTE.—(1) The above amounts of drawing rights are based in part on estimates by the Bizone of coal exports.

If these figures are altered during the year ending 30 October 1948, adjustments may be necessary as outlined in paragraph 7 of the Council Decision on 11 September 1948 on the division of direct aid and redistribution of Contributions and drawing rights (Doc. No. C [48] 158).

(2) The figures inserted for the United Kingdom cover also the countries (including Iceland and Ireland) which comprise the sterling area, that is to say, the 'Scheduled Territories' as defined for exchange control purposes in United Kingdom legislation.

PROTOCOL OF PROVISIONAL APPLICATION OF THE AGREEMENT FOR INTRA-EUROPEAN PAYMENTS AND COMPENSATIONS

Paris, 16 October 1948

The Signatories of the Agreement for Intra-European Payments and Multilateral Compensations signed this day, (hereinafter referred to as the Agreement);

Desiring to give immediate and provisional effect to the Agreement;

Have agreed as follows:—

(1) The Parties to the present Protocol shall apply the provisions of the Agreement provisionally as if the Agreement had been effective on and after 1 October 1948.

(2) The present Protocol shall come into force on this day's date and shall continue in force until the Agreement comes into force.

(3) (a) Any Party to the present Protocol may withdraw from the Protocol by giving not less than three months' notice of withdrawal in writing to the Secretary-General of the Organization for European Economic Co-operation (hereinafter referred to as the Secretary-General).

(b) Three months after the date on which such notice is given, or at such later time as may be specified in the notice, the Party giving it shall cease to be a Party to the present Protocol.

(c) The Secretary-General will immediately inform all Parties to the present Protocol and the Agent of any notice given under this paragraph.

(4) If notice of withdrawal is given under paragraph (3), the Parties to the present Protocol, acting through the Organization, shall, at the request of any Party, entrust a Committee or Committees with the preparation of recommendations as to the provisions which may be required to avoid,

(i) interruptions in trade or payments,

(ii) payments of gold or foreign currency,

(iii) the prevention of repurchase of gold or foreign currency which would otherwise have been possible under the provisions of the Agreement, or

(iv) other similar possible consequences,

which may arise, within a reasonable time from the date when the notice of withdrawal takes effect, as a result of changes in balances caused by compensations made under the Agreement. The Committee or Committees shall also consider the position of drawing rights which may remain unused at the date on which the notice of withdrawal takes effect.

In witness whereof, the undersigned Plenipotentiaries, duly empowered, have appended their signatures to the present Protocol.

Done in Paris this 16 October 1948, in the English and French languages, both texts being equally authentic, in a single copy which shall remain deposited with the Secretary-General of the Organization for European Economic Co-operation by which certified copies shall be communicated to all the signatories to the present Protocol.

DECISION OF THE COUNCIL ON THE APPLICATION OF CERTAIN PRINCIPLES OF COMMERCIAL POLICY

The Council:

Taking into consideration Article 11 of the Convention for European Economic Co-operation dated on 16 April 1948, which lays down that: 'The aim of the Organization shall be the achievement of a sound European economy through the economic co-operation of its members. An immediate task of the Organization will be to ensure the success of the European recovery programme, in accordance with the undertakings contained in Part I of the present Convention', and

Taking into consideration Article 13 of the said Convention which lays down that: 'In order to achieve its aim as set out in Article 11 the Organization may: (a) take decisions for implementation by members', and

Having regard to the introduction of the plan for intra-European payments and compensations and the circumstances in which it is being introduced;

Hereby decides:—

(i) To call upon members to implement the recommendations in respect of certain principles of commercial policy annexed hereto.

(ii) This decision shall have effect as from the date of signature of the Agreement for Intra-European Payments and Compensations recommended this day by the Council for signature and shall be binding only as between the members which are bound to apply the provisions of the said Agreement for as long as they are so bound.

ANNEX

GENERAL RECOMMENDATIONS FOR CERTAIN PRINCIPLES OF COMMERCIAL POLICY DURING THE CURRENCY OF THE INTRA-EUROPEAN PAYMENTS SCHEME

(1) In general, it is important that the new resources to be made available to participating countries under the intra-European payments scheme should be used wisely and to the maximum advantage of the participating countries taken as a whole. Further, it is desir-

able that the development of trade should be along lines which will facilitate orderly progress towards multilateral trading. It is therefore necessary that the commercial policies followed by the participating countries should aim both at a restoration of their external equilibrium and at a rationalization as well as an increase in the flow of intra-European trade, within the framework of the long-term objectives of the Organization.

(2) In particular, the use of the new resources to be made available to participating countries under the intra-European payments scheme is intended to enable debtor countries, to the full extent practicable, to buy under reasonable commercial conditions goods necessary for their recovery.

(3) The Council agrees that, at this stage, it would not be advisable to go beyond the formulation of certain principles for the guidance of participating countries in their commercial relations with other participating countries.

(4) The participating countries fall into three groups:

(*a*) Countries which are in substantial surplus (on their balance of payments on current account) with the other participating countries taken as a whole. For convenience, these countries will be referred to in this paper as 'net creditor countries'.

(*b*) Countries which are in substantial deficit (on their balance of payments on current account) with other participating countries taken as a whole. For convenience these will be referred to in this paper as 'net debtor countries'.

(*c*) Countries which are more or less in balance. For convenience, these will be referred to in this paper as 'intermediate countries'.

(5) The fundamental task of participating countries, as stated in Article IV of the Convention for European Economic Co-operation, is that they should collectively and individually, correct or avoid excessive disequilibrium in their financial and economic relations, both among themselves and with non-participating countries. The Council wish to make it clear that the recommendations made in paragraph 6 below have been formulated, and must be applied, with due regard to these objectives.

(6) In order to attain conditions favourable for the achievement of the objectives set out in paragraphs 1 and 5, the Council recommends that, subject to any modifications necessary to conform to any particular policies recommended by O.E.E.C., the following policies should be pursued during the currency of the intra-European payments scheme.

(i) All countries should seek to increase their trade in order to reach a satisfactory level of economic activity with a view to facilitating their recovery.

(ii) All countries should maintain normal exports necessary to the recovery of other participating countries and each should do its best to increase such exports, if this would enable other participating countries to obtain in Europe goods which are otherwise obtainable only for dollars, provided that such an increase would not prejudice the exporting country's recovery programme.

(iii) Net debtor countries and intermediate countries should do their best to increase their current exports to net creditor countries in order to reduce the disequilibrium as much and as quickly as possible. To this end, net debtor countries and intermediate countries should in respect of exports to net creditor countries take similar steps to those they are taking in respect of current exports to any other country, although they should not be expected to have to accord to the net creditor countries such priorities as may be accorded to exports to countries with whom they have special relations, including those between a metropolitan country and its associated territories.

(iv) Net creditor countries and intermediate countries should buy from net debtor countries additional goods and services as freely as is reasonably practicable in order to reduce the disequilibrium. So far as the export of goods not necessary for the recovery of net debtor countries is concerned, net creditor and intermediate countries should follow a policy which would help the net debtor countries in their efforts to reduce the disequilibrium.

(v) Net creditor countries should buy from intermediate countries, for the purpose of safeguarding the latters' equilibrium, additional goods and services as freely as is reasonably practicable. So far as the export of goods not necessary for the recovery of intermediate countries is concerned, net creditor countries should follow a policy which would help the intermediate countries in their efforts to safeguard their equilibrium.

(vi) Net creditor countries will facilitate the use of the new resources to be made available under the intra-European payments scheme for the purchase of goods necessary for recovery. More particularly, net creditor and other participating countries should do their best to increase their exports to other participating countries of products whose procurement within the group of participating countries may be understood between the countries concerned, or may be considered by the Organization, to be necessary as a result of decisions taken by the Organization with respect to the distribution of aid.

It is not intended that the application of these principles should jeopardize a vital economic interest in any participating country.

(vii) Net debtor countries should exercise, in their external expenditure, the maximum of economy compatible with their economic recovery.

(7) No attempt has been made at this stage, apart from paragraph 6 (i) and (ii), to formulate general principles for the commercial relations of net creditor countries with each other, or of net debtor countries with each other, or of intermediate countries with each other. It is hoped that the appropriate pattern of trade may be expected to emerge in these cases, if the recommendations in paragraph 6 are followed in respect of the cases in that paragraph.

(8) The Council therefore invites the participating countries to examine whether the commercial policies pursued by them during the currency of the intra-European payments scheme are in accordance with the recommendations in paragraph 6; and to inform the Organization, in time for a further report to the Council by a date to be fixed by the latter, of the result of this examination and of such modifications as they may have made, or may propose to make, in respect of their import and export policy in conformity with these recommendations.

(9) The Council recommends also that O.E.E.C. should keep under general review the implementation of the recommendations in paragraph 6, and that it should be open to any participating country to call the attention of O.E.E.C. to instances in which, in its opinion, the recommendations are not being followed.

(10) The foregoing provisions are not intended to modify the application of the existing trade agreements between the participating countries, save for possibilities for adjustment by mutual agreement.

FRANCO-ITALIAN CUSTOMS TREATY[1]

Paris, 26 March 1949

The President of the French Republic and the President of the Italian Republic, having regard to the declaration, dated 13 September 1947, whereby the French Government and the Italian Government affirmed their desire to examine the basis on which it might be possible to establish a Customs Union between the two countries, with the principal aims of ensuring a reduction of production costs and selling prices, a higher standard of living, and full employment of labour;

Having regard to the favourable conclusions reached, in its report on 22 December 1947, by the Franco-Italian Mixed Commission which was entrusted with that investigation;

Having regard to the protocol signed at Turin on 20 March 1948 wherein the two Governments confirmed the aforesaid conclusions and declared their formal desire to establish a Franco-Italian Customs Union;

Having regard to the report of 22 January 1949 produced by the Franco-Italian Mixed Commission entrusted, under the Turin protocol, with drawing up the plan and programme putting into effect the aforesaid Union:

Having regard to the final act of the United Nations Conference on Trade and Employment, dated 24 March 1948, of which France and Italy are signatories, and having regard also to Article 44 of the Havana Charter;

Have decided to set in motion the necessary dispositions for the establishment of a Customs Union regime, and to this end have designated as their plenipotentiaries:

For the President of the French Republic, M. Robert Schuman, Minister of Foreign Affairs; for the President of the Italian Republic, Count Carlo Sforza, Minister of Foreign Affairs; who, having exchanged their full powers, recognized in good and due form, have agreed to the following dispositions:

Article 1

A Customs Union is established between Metropolitan France together with the departments of Algeria of the one part, and Italy of the other part.

[1] *Relazioni Internazionali*, 3 April 1949. (*Translation.*)

TARIFF UNION

Article 2

Within the period of one year from the date of the coming into force of the present treaty a common Customs tariff shall be applied on the foreign frontiers of the Union, in conformity with legislation and uniform regulations to be established.

Article 3

Dating from the coming into force of the aforesaid tariff, no Customs duty shall be charged on national or nationalized goods coming from one of the territories of the Union and imported into the other. As from the same date, no export Customs duty shall be charged on national or nationalized goods exported from one of the territories of the Union and destined for the other.

Article 4

Until the equalization of the fiscal burdens in the two countries has been put into effect, the goods referred to in the preceding article shall benefit, in the exporting territory, by the waiver or repayment of the taxes or internal dues collected on behalf of the State, whereas in the importing territory such goods will continue to be subject to the payment of taxes and dues other than Customs duties.

Article 5

The division of the Customs proceeds between the two countries shall be regulated by a subsequent agreement.

ECONOMIC UNION

Article 6

From the coming into force of the present treaty, there shall be put into effect all those measures suitable for the development of econo-mic relations between France and Italy, which may further the achievement of economic union between the two countries. Restriction of movement of goods and persons between the two countries shall be gradually abolished in proportion as harmony is achieved between the legislation of the two countries, in accordance with Article 15, paragraph 2. The organ envisaged in Article 9 shall, within two years from its beginning to function, put forward practicable proposals as to the period within which the economic Union shall be completely brought into effect; the two High Contracting Parties hope that this period will not exceed six years.

Article 7

Beginning with the coming into force of the present treaty, and during the period envisaged under Article 6, compensatory measures can be applied in respect of the goods mentioned in Article 3; such measures to consist principally of taxes introduced as an exceptional and temporary step by one or other of the two Governments. Such measures shall be directed either towards compensating for the difference of burdens resulting from the disparity between the respective legislations, until such time as the latter are harmonized; or towards normalizing and alleviating the effects of the suppression of the quantitative restrictions. The combined effect of the aforesaid measures shall be to bring the resulting protection to a lower level than that at present in existence in respect of the same goods coming from third-party states.

Article 8

The two Governments will be enabled to maintain in existence the monopolies established by them and at present in force.

COUNCIL OF THE CUSTOMS UNION

Article 9

A common organ, to be known as the 'Council of the Franco-Italian Customs Union', shall be set up within a month of the coming into force of the present treaty. It shall be composed, on each side, of a Delegate General, an Assistant Delegate General, and seven members chosen according to their specific competence. A mixed administrative secretariat shall be set up, whose members shall be appointed by joint nomination of the two Delegate Generals. The expenses involved in its functioning are to be borne in equal parts by each of the two Governments.

Article 10

The Council shall meet at regular intervals. Extraordinary sessions can take place upon the initiative of one or other of the Delegate Generals. The Presidency shall be held alternately, for a period of one year, by one or other of the two Delegate Generals. The Council's deliberations shall not be valid unless at least two-thirds of the members of each delegation are present. It will decide on its own internal regulations and will establish the organization and procedure for its own labours.

Article 11

The Council shall set up specialized mixed Commissions to examine the various particular problems resulting from the operation of the Union. Such Commissions shall be dependent on the Council, which shall determine their composition and competence. The members of the Commissions can be either representatives of the administrations of each of the two States, or experts, nominated by the Governments, either directly or on the proposal of economic or specialized organizations.

Article 12

Each Delegate General shall have accredited to the delegation of the other country a representative whose function is to ensure liaison between the two delegations. This representative shall be appointed by the Government on the proposal of its Delegate General.

Article 13

A permanent section of the Council, composed of the two Assistant Delegate Generals, of delegates chosen by them in common agreement, and of the two representatives mentioned in the preceding article, shall meet at intervals to be decided by the Council, and, if necessary, more frequently. Experts can also be called upon to take part in these meetings.

Article 14

The permanent section shall examine and co-ordinate the labours of the special Commissions, and shall present to each session of the Council reports on the questions appearing on the agenda, and also, if necessary, on any other question which it may consider opportune to bring to the attention of the Council.

Article 15

The Council—all powers of decision and execution being still reserved to the respective Governments—shall have the following powers:—

(i) to prepare a tariff union and to superintend its being put into effect within the period laid down in Article 2;

(ii) to prepare the economic union and superintend its coming into effect. To this end the Council, on 1 October of each year, beginning with 1 October 1949, shall submit to the two Governments the programme of measures to be undertaken in the course of the coming year, and also the texts to be approved to ensure the realization of the Union, especially by means of harmonising legislation on agriculture, industry, social affairs, and fiscal, monetary, and Customs matters, and, in general, economic legislation of any kind;

(iii) to further any useful proposal directed principally towards effecting: the most rational and extensive use of manpower, with a view to raising the standard of living of both peoples; the development of commercial activity in each of the two countries in furtherance of the interest of the Union; the adoption of measures calculated to intensify trade exchanges both between the two countries and with third-party States;

(iv) to facilitate, supervise, and orientate all the relations which the establishment of the Union will create and develop with administrations, public bodies, and specialized organizations in the two countries;

(v) to express an opinion on measures submitted to it by one or other of the two Governments. In particular, the measures outlined in Article 7 shall, through the medium of one or other of the two Governments, be submitted to the opinion of the Council. In this connection the latter can put forward recommendations to the two Governments, especially regarding the duration, continuance, modification, or suppression of these measures.

Article 16

The Delegate General of each of the two countries shall ensure liaison between his own Government and the Council. To this end he shall make known the Council's proposals to his own Government, keep the Council informed of the progress of these proposals, submit to it requests for an opinion on behalf of his Government, and transmit replies to the latter. He shall follow all questions relating to the Customs Union, and his Government is compulsorily obliged to consult him on all such questions.

FINAL CLAUSES

Article 17

All disputes relating to the interpretation of the present treaty which are not settled by direct negotiations shall be regulated through an arbitral procedure the methods of which shall be established by common agreement for each individual case.

Article 18

The present treaty, drawn up in two copies, one in French and the other in Italian, shall be ratified according to the constitutional practice of each of the two States. It shall come into force from the date of the exchange of ratifications.

NORTH ATLANTIC TREATY.[1] TEXT PROPOSED FOR SIGNATURE DURING THE FIRST WEEK OF APRIL 1949

PREAMBLE

The Parties to this Treaty reaffirm their faith in the purposes and principles of the Charter of the United Nations[2] and their desire to live in peace with all peoples and all Governments.

They are determined to safeguard the freedom, common heritage and civilization of their peoples, founded on the principles of democracy, individual liberty and the rule of law.

They seek to promote stability and well-being in the North Atlantic area.

They are resolved to unite their efforts for collective defence for the preservation of peace and security.

They therefore agree to this North Atlantic Treaty.

Article 1

The Parties undertake, as set forth in the Charter of the United Nations, to settle any international disputes in which they may be involved by peaceful means in such a manner that international peace and security and justice are not endangered, and to refrain in their international relations from the threat or use of force in any manner inconsistent with the purposes of the United Nations.

Article 2

The Parties will contribute toward the further development of peaceful and friendly international relations by strengthening their free institutions, by bringing about a better understanding of the principles upon which these institutions are founded, and by promoting conditions of stability and well-being. They will seek to eliminate conflict in their international economic policies and will encourage economic collaboration between any or all of them.

Article 3

In order more effectively to achieve the objectives of this Treaty, the Parties, separately and jointly, by means of continuous and effective self-help and mutual aid, will maintain and develop their individual and collective capacity to resist armed attack.

[1] Cmd. 7657.
[2] 'Treaty Series No. 67 (1946),' Cmd. 7015.

Article 4

The Parties will consult together whenever, in the opinion of any of them, the territorial integrity, political independence or security of any of the Parties is threatened.

Article 5

The Parties agree that an armed attack against one or more of them in Europe or North America shall be considered an attack against them all and consequently they agree that, if such an armed attack occurs, each of them, in exercise of the right of individual or collective self-defence recognized by Article 51 of the Charter of the United Nations, will assist the Party or Parties so attacked by taking forthwith, individually and in concert with the other Parties, such action as it deems necessary, including the use of armed force, to restore and maintain the security of the North Atlantic area.

Any such armed attack and all measures taken as a result thereof shall immediately be reported to the Security Council. Such measures shall be terminated when the Security Council has taken the measures necessary to restore and maintain international peace and security.

Article 6

For the purpose of Article 5 an armed attack on one or more of the Parties is deemed to include an armed attack on the territory of any of the Parties in Europe or North America, on the Algerian Departments of France, on the occupation forces of any Party in Europe, on the islands under the jurisdiction of any Party in the North Atlantic area north of the Tropic of Cancer or on the vessels or aircraft in this area of any of the Parties.

Article 7

This Treaty does not affect, and shall not be interpreted as affecting, in any way the rights and obligations under the Charter of the Parties which are members of the United Nations, or the primary responsibility of the Security Council for the maintenance of international peace and security.

Article 8

Each Party declares that none of the international engagements now in force between it and any other of the Parties or any third State is in conflict with the provisions of this Treaty, and undertakes not to enter into any international engagement in conflict with this Treaty.

Article 9

The Parties hereby establish a Council, on which each of them shall be represented, to consider matters concerning the implementation of this Treaty. The Council shall be so organized as to be able to meet promptly at any time. The Council shall set up such subsidiary bodies as may be necessary; in particular it shall establish immediately a Defence Committee which shall recommend measures for the implementation of Articles 3 and 5.

Article 10

The Parties may, by unanimous agreement, invite any other European State in a position to further the principles of this Treaty and to contribute to the security of the North Atlantic area to accede to this Treaty. Any State so invited may become a Party to the Treaty by depositing its instrument of accession with the Government of the United States of America.

The Government of the United States of America will inform each of the Parties of the deposit of each such instrument of accession.

Article 11

This Treaty shall be ratified and its provisions carried out by the Parties in accordance with their respective constitutional processes. The instruments of ratification shall be deposited as soon as possible with the Government of the United States of America, which will notify all the other signatories of each deposit. The Treaty shall enter into force between the States which have ratified it as soon as the ratifications of the majority of the signatories, including the ratifications of Belgium, Canada, France, Luxembourg, the Netherlands, the United Kingdom and the United States, have been deposited and shall come into effect with respect to other States on the date of the deposit of their ratifications.

Article 12

After the Treaty has been in force for ten years, or at any time thereafter, the Parties shall, if any of them so requests, consult together for the purpose of reviewing the Treaty, having regard for the factors then affecting peace and security in the North Atlantic area, including the development of universal as well as regional arrangements under the Charter of the United Nations for the maintenance of international peace and security.

Article 13

After the Treaty has been in force for twenty years, any Party may cease to be a Party one year after its notice of denunciation has been given to the Government of the United States of America, which will inform the Governments of the other Parties of the deposit of each notice of denunciation.

Article 14

This Treaty, of which the English and French texts are equally authentic, shall be deposited in the archives of the Government of the United States of America. Duly certified copies thereof will be transmitted by that Government to the Governments of the other signatories.

In witness whereof, the undersigned Plenipotentiaries have signed this Treaty.

Done at Washington, the   day of April 1949.

NOTE

The Text of this Treaty as signed at Washington on 4 April 1949 is exactly as given above, but it had not been officially printed by His Majesty's Stationery Office when this collection of documents was sent to press.

STATUTE OF THE COUNCIL OF EUROPE[1]

London, 5 May 1949

The Governments of the Kingdom of Belgium, the Kingdom of Denmark, the French Republic, the Irish Republic, the Italian Republic, the Grand Duchy of Luxembourg, the Kingdom of the Netherlands, the Kingdom of Norway, the Kingdom of Sweden, and the United Kingdom of Great Britain and Northern Ireland;

Convinced that the pursuit of peace based upon justice and international co-operation is vital for the preservation of human society and civilization;

Reaffirming their devotion to the spiritual and moral values which are the common heritage of their peoples and the true source of individual freedom, political liberty and the rule of law, principles which form the basis of all genuine democracy;

Believing that, for the maintenance and further realization of these ideals and i.. ' e interests of economic and social progress, there is need of a closer unity between all like-minded countries of Europe;

Considering that, to respond to this need and to the expressed aspirations of their peoples in this regard, it is necessary forthwith to create an organization which will bring European States into closer association;

Have in consequence decided to set up a Council of Europe consisting of a Committee of representatives of Governments and of a Consultative Assembly, and have for this purpose adopted the following Statute:—

CHAPTER I—AIM OF THE COUNCIL OF EUROPE

Article 1

(*a*) The aim of the Council of Europe is to achieve a greater unity between its Members for the purpose of safeguarding and realizing the ideals and principles which are their common heritage and facilitating their economic and social progress.

(*b*) This aim shall be pursued through the organs of the Council by discussion of questions of common concern and by agreements and common action in economic, social, cultural, scientific, legal, and administrative matters and in the maintenance and further realization of human rights and fundamental freedoms.

(*c*) Participation in the Council of Europe shall not affect the

[1] Cmd. 7686.

collaboration of its Members in the work of the United Nations and of other international organizations or unions to which they are parties.

(d) Matters relating to National Defence do not fall within the scope of the Council of Europe.

CHAPTER II—MEMBERSHIP

Article 2

The Members of the Council of Europe are the Parties to this Statute.

Article 3

Every Member of the Council of Europe must accept the principles of the rule of law and of the enjoyment by all persons within its jurisdiction of human rights and fundamental freedoms, and collaborate sincerely and effectively in the realization of the aim of the Council as specified in Chapter I.

Article 4

Any European State, which is deemed to be able and willing to fulfil the provisions of Article 3, may be invited to become a Member of the Council of Europe by the Committee of Ministers. Any State so invited shall become a Member on the deposit on its behalf with the Secretary-General of an instrument of accession to the present Statute.

Article 5

(a) In special circumstances, a European country, which is deemed to be able and willing to fulfil the provisions of Article 3, may be invited by the Committee of Ministers to become an Associate Member of the Council of Europe. Any country so invited shall become an Associate Member on the deposit on its behalf with the Secretary-General of an instrument accepting the present Statute. An Associate Member shall be entitled to be represented in the Consultative Assembly only.

(b) The expression 'Member' in this Statute includes an Associate Member except when used in connection with representation on the Committee of Ministers.

Article 6

Before issuing invitations under Articles 4 or 5 above, the Committee of Ministers shall determine the number of representatives on the Consultative Assembly to which the proposed Member shall be entitled and its proportionate financial contribution.

Article 7

Any Member of the Council of Europe may withdraw by formally notifying the Secretary-General of its intention to do so. Such withdrawal shall take effect at the end of the financial year in which it is notified, if the notification is given during the first nine months of that financial year. If the notification is given in the last three months of the financial year, it shall take effect at the end of the next financial year.

Article 8

Any Member of the Council of Europe, which has seriously violated Article 3, may be suspended from its rights of representation and requested by the Committee of Ministers to withdraw under Article 7. If such Member does not comply with this request, the Committee may decide that it has ceased to be a Member of the Council as from such date as the Committee may determine.

Article 9

The Committee of Ministers may suspend the right of representation on the Committee and on the Consultative Assembly of a member, which has failed to fulfil its financial obligation, during such period as the obligation remains unfulfilled.

CHAPTER III—GENERAL

Article 10

The organs of the Council of Europe are:
 (i) the Committee of Ministers;
 (ii) the Consultative Assembly.
Both these organs shall be served by the Secretariat of the Council of Europe.

Article 11

The seat of the Council of Europe is at Strasbourg.

Article 12

The official languages of the Council of Europe are English and French. The rules of procedure of the Committee of Ministers and of the Consultative Assembly shall determine in what circumstances and under what conditions other languages may be used.

CHAPTER IV—COMMITTEE OF MINISTERS

Article 13

The Committee of Ministers is the organ which acts on behalf of the Council of Europe in accordance with Articles 15 and 16.

142

Article 14

Each Member shall be entitled to one representative on the Committee of Ministers and each representative shall be entitled to one vote. Representatives on the Committee shall be the Ministers for Foreign Affairs. When a Minister for Foreign Affairs is unable to be present, or in other circumstances where it may be desirable, an alternate may be nominated to act for him, who shall, whenever possible, be a member of his Government.

Article 15

(*a*) On the recommendation of the Consultative Assembly or on its own initiative, the Committee of Ministers shall consider the action required to further the aim of the Council of Europe, including the conclusion of conventions or agreements and the adoption by Governments of a common policy with regard to particular matters. Its conclusions shall be communicated to members by the Secretary-General.

(*b*) In appropriate cases, the conclusions of the Committee may take the form of recommendations to the Governments of Members, and the Committee may request the Governments of Members to inform it of the action taken by them with regard to such recommendations.

Article 16

The Committee of Ministers shall, subject to the provisions of Articles 24, 28, 30, 32, 33, and 35, relating to the powers of the Consultative Assembly, decide with binding effect all matters relating to the internal organization and arrangements of the Council of Europe. For this purpose the Committee of Ministers shall adopt such financial and administrative regulations as may be necessary.

Article 17

The Committee of Ministers may set up advisory and technical committees or commissions for such specific purposes as it may deem desirable.

Article 18

The Committee of Ministers shall adopt its rules of procedure which shall determine amongst other things:
  (i)   the quorum;
  (ii) the method of appointment and term of office of its President;
  (iii) the procedure for the admission of items to its agenda, including the giving of notice of proposals for resolutions; and
  (iv) the notifications required for the nomination of alternates under Article 14.

143

Article 19

At each session of the Consultative Assembly the Committee of Ministers shall furnish the Assembly with statements of its activities, accompanied by appropriate documentation.

Article 20

(*a*) Resolutions of the Committee of Ministers relating to the following important matters—namely:

    (i) recommendations under Article 15 (*b*);
    (ii) questions under Article 19;
    (iii) questions under Article 21 (*a*) (i) and (*b*);
    (iv) questions under Article 33;
    (v) recommendations for the amendment of Articles 1 (*d*), 7, 15, 20, and 22; and
    (vi) any other question which the Committee may, by a resolution passed under (*d*) below, decide should be subject to a unanimous vote on account of its importance

require the unanimous vote of the representatives casting a vote, and of a majority of the representatives entitled to sit on the Committee.

(*b*) Questions arising under the rules of procedure or under the financial and administrative regulations may be decided by a simple majority vote of the representatives entitled to sit on the Committee.

(*c*) Resolutions of the Committee under Articles 4 and 5 require a two-thirds majority of all the representatives entitled to sit on the Committee.

(*d*) All other resolutions of the Committee, including the adoption of the Budget, of rules of procedure and of financial and administrative regulations, recommendations for the amendment of articles of this Statute, other than those mentioned in paragraph (*a*) (v) above, and deciding in case of doubt which paragraph of this Article applies, require a two-thirds majority of the representatives casting a vote and of a majority of the representatives entitled to sit on the Committee.

Article 21

(*a*) Unless the Committee decides otherwise, meetings of the Committee of Ministers shall be held—(i) in private, and (ii) at the seat of the Council.

(*b*) The Committee shall determine what information shall be published regarding the conclusions and discussions of a meeting held in private.

(*c*) The Committee shall meet before and during the beginning of every session of the Consultative Assembly and at such other times as it may decide.

CHAPTER V—THE CONSULTATIVE ASSEMBLY

Article 22

The Consultative Assembly is the deliberative organ of the Council of Europe. It shall debate matters within its competence under this Statute and present its conclusions, in the form of recommendations, to the Committee of Ministers.

Article 23

(a) The Consultative Assembly shall discuss, and may make recommendations upon, any matter within the aim and scope of the Council of Europe as defined in Chapter I, which (i) is referred to it by the Committee of Ministers with a request for its opinion, or (ii) has been approved by the Committee for inclusion in the Agenda of the Assembly on the proposal of the latter.

(b) In taking decisions under (a), the Committee shall have regard to the work of other European inter-governmental organizations to which some or all of the Members of the Council are parties.

(c) The President of the Assembly shall decide, in case of doubt, whether any question raised in the course of the Session is within the Agenda of the Assembly approved under (a) above.

Article 24

The Consultative Assembly may, with due regard to the provisions of Article 38 (d), establish committees or commissions to consider and report to it on any matter which falls within its competence under Article 23, to examine and prepare questions on its agenda and to advise on all matters of procedure.

Article 25

(a) The Consultative Assembly shall consist of representatives of each Member appointed in such a manner as the Government of that Member shall decide. Each representative must be a national of the Member whom he represents, but shall not at the same time be a member of the Committee of Ministers.

(b) No representative shall be deprived of his position as such during a session of the Assembly without the agreement of the Assembly.

(c) Each representative may have a substitute who may, in the absence of the representative, sit, speak, and vote in his place. The provisions of paragraph (a) above apply to the appointment of substitutes.

Article 26

The following States, on becoming Members, shall be entitled to the number of representatives given below:—Belgium 6, Denmark 4,

France 18, Irish Republic 4, Italy 18, Luxembourg 3, Netherlands 6, Norway 4, Sweden 6, United Kingdom 18.

Article 27

The conditions under which the Committee of Ministers collectively may be represented in the debates of the Consultative Assembly, or individual representatives on the Committee may address the Assembly, shall be determined by such rules of procedure on this subject as may be drawn up by the Committee after consultation with the Assembly.

Article 28

(a) The Consultative Assembly shall adopt its rules of procedure and shall elect from its members its President, who shall remain in office until the next ordinary session.

(b) The President shall control the proceedings but shall not take part in the debate or vote. The substitute of the representative who is President may sit, speak, and vote in his place.

(c) The rules of procedure shall determine *inter alia*:
   (i) the quorum;
   (ii) the manner of the election and terms of office of the President and other officers;
   (iii) the manner in which the agenda shall be drawn up and be communicated to representatives; and
   (iv) the time and manner in which the names of representatives and their substitutes shall be notified.

Article 29

Subject to the provisions of Article 30, all resolutions of the Consultative Assembly, including resolutions:
   (i) embodying recommendations to the Committee of Ministers;
   (ii) proposing to the Committee matters for discussion in the assembly;
   (iii) establishing committees or commissions;
   (iv) determining the date of commencement of its sessions;
   (v) determining what majority is required for resolutions in cases not covered by (i) to (iv) above or determining cases of doubt as to what majority is required,

shall require a two-thirds majority of the representatives casting a vote.

Article 30

On matters relating to its internal procedure, which includes the election of officers, the nomination of persons to serve on committees and commissions and the adoption of rules of procedure, resolutions of the Consultative Assembly shall be carried by such majorities as the Assembly may determine in accordance with Article 29 (v).

Article 31

Debates on proposals to be made to the Committee of Ministers that a matter should be placed on the Agenda of the Consultative Assembly shall be confined to an indication of the proposed subject-matter and the reasons for and against its inclusion in the Agenda.

Article 32

The Consultative Assembly shall meet in ordinary session once a year, the date and duration of which shall be determined by the Assembly so as to avoid as far as possible overlapping with parliamentary sessions of Members and with sessions of the General Assembly of the United Nations. In no circumstances shall the duration of an ordinary session exceed one month unless both the Assembly and the Committee of Ministers concur.

Article 33

Ordinary sessions of the Consultative Assembly shall be held at the seat of the Council unless both the Assembly and the Committee of Ministers concur that it should be held elsewhere.

Article 34

The Committee of Ministers may convoke an extraordinary session of the Consultative Assembly at such time and place as the Committee, with the concurrence of the President of the Assembly, shall decide.

Article 35

Unless the Consultative Assembly decides otherwise, its debates shall be conducted in public.

CHAPTER VI—THE SECRETARIAT

Article 36

(a) The Secretariat shall consist of a Secretary-General, a Deputy Secretary-General and such other staff as may be required.

(b) The Secretary-General and Deputy Secretary-General shall be appointed by the Consultative Assembly on the recommendation of the Committee of Ministers.

(c) The remaining staff of the Secretariat shall be appointed by the Secretary-General, in accordance with the administrative regulations.

(d) No member of the Secretariat shall hold any salaried office from any Government or be a member of the Consultative Assembly or of any national legislature or engage in any occupation incompatible with his duties.

(e) Every member of the staff of the Secretariat shall make a solemn declaration affirming that his duty is to the Council of Europe and that he will perform his duties conscientiously, uninfluenced by any national considerations, and that he will not seek or receive instructions in connection with the performance of his duties from any Government or any authority external to the Council and will refrain from any action which might reflect on his position as an international official responsible only to the Council. In the case of the Secretary-General and the Deputy Secretary-General this declaration shall be made before the Committee, and in the case of all other members of the staff, before the Secretary-General.

(f) Every Member shall respect the exclusively international character of the responsibilities of the Secretary-General and the staff of the Secretariat and not seek to influence them in the discharge of their responsibilities.

Article 37

(a) The Secretariat shall be located at the seat of the Council.

(b) The Secretary-General is responsible to the Committee of Ministers for the work of the Secretariat. Amongst other things, he shall, subject to Article 38 (d), provide such secretarial and other assistance as the Consultative Assembly may require.

CHAPTER VII—FINANCE

Article 38

(a) Each Member shall bear the expenses of its own representation in the Committee of Ministers and in the Consultative Assembly.

(b) The expenses of the Secretariat and a.. .:... common expenses shall be shared between all Members in such proportions as shall be determined by the Committee on the basis of the population of Members.

The contributions of an Associate Member shall be determined by the Committee.

(c) In accordance with the financial regulations, the Budget of the Council shall be submitted annually by the Secretary-General for adoption by the Committee.

(d) The Secretary-General shall refer to the Committee requests from the Assembly which involve expenditure exceeding the amount already allocated in the Budget for the Assembly and its activities.

148

Article 39

The Secretary-General shall each year notify the Government of each Member of the amount of its contribution and each Member shall pay to the Secretary-General the amount of its contribution, which shall be deemed to be due on the date of its notification, not later than six months after that date.

CHAPTER VIII—PRIVILEGES AND IMMUNITIES

Article 40

(*a*) The Council of Europe, representatives of Members and the Secretariat shall enjoy in the territories of its Members such privileges and immunities as are reasonably necessary for the fulfilment of their functions. These immunities shall include immunity for all representatives in the Consultative Assembly from arrest and all legal proceedings in the territories of all Members, in respect of words spoken and votes cast in the debates of the Assembly or its committees or commissions.

(*b*) The Members undertake as soon as possible to enter into an agreement for the purpose of fulfilling the provisions of paragraph (*a*) above. For this purpose the Committee of Ministers shall recommend to the Governments of Members the acceptance of an Agreement defining the privileges and immunities to be granted in the territories of all Members. In addition a special Agreement shall be concluded with the Government of the French Republic defining the privileges and immunities which the Council shall enjoy at its seat.

CHAPTER IX—AMENDMENTS

Article 41

(*a*) Proposals for the amendment of this Statute may be made in the Committee of Ministers or, in the conditions provided for in Article 23, in the Consultative Assembly.

(*b*) The Committee shall recommend and cause to be embodied in a Protocol those amendments which it considers to be desirable.

(*c*) An amending Protocol shall come into force when it has been signed and ratified on behalf of two-thirds of the Members.

(*d*) Notwithstanding the provisions of the preceding paragraphs of this Article, amendments to Articles 23–35, 38, and 39 which have been approved by the Committee and by the Assembly shall come into force on the date of the certificate of the Secretary-General, transmitted to the Governments of Members, certifying that they have been so approved. This paragraph shall not operate until the conclusion of the second ordinary session of the Assembly.

CHAPTER X—FINAL PROVISIONS

Article 42

(a) This Statute shall be ratified. Ratifications shall be deposited with the Government of the United Kingdom of Great Britain and Northern Ireland.

(b) The present Statute shall come into force as soon as seven instruments of ratification have been deposited. The Government of the United Kingdom shall transmit to all signatory Governments a certificate declaring that the Statute has entered into force, and giving the names of the Members of the Council of Europe on that date.

(c) Thereafter each other signatory shall become a party to this Statute as from the date of the deposit of its instrument of ratification.

In witness whereof the undersigned, being duly authorized thereto, have signed the present Statute.

Done at London, this fifth day of May, 1949, in English and French, both texts being equally authentic, in a single copy which shall remain deposited in the archives of the Government of the United Kingdom which shall transmit certified copies to the other signatory Governments.

[*Here follow the Signatures*]